Criminal Justice
Recent Scholarship

Edited by
Marilyn McShane and Frank P. Williams III

A Series from LFB Scholarly

Juvenile Arrest in America
Race, Social Class, and Gang Membership

Mike Tapia

LFB Scholarly Publishing LLC
El Paso 2012

Library of Congress Cataloging-in-Publication Data

Tapia, Mike, 1974-
  Juvenile arrest in America : race, social class, and gang membership /
Mike Tapia.
      p. cm.
  Includes bibliographical references and index.
  ISBN 978-1-59332-478-0 (hardcover : alk. paper)
  1. Juvenile delinquency--United States. 2. Juvenile justice,
Administration of--United States. 3. Discrimination in criminal justice
administration--Utah. 4. Gangs--United States. I. Title.
  HV9104.T35 2012
  364.360973--dc23
                                              2011038028

ISBN 978-1-59332-478-0

Printed on acid-free 250-year-life paper.

Manufactured in the United States of America.

Table of Contents

List of Tables   **vii**

List of Figures   **ix**

CHAPTER 1: Introduction and Theoretical Background 1
Framework   2
Labeling and Conflict Theories   3
Conflict-Based Components of Labeling   5
Interaction Effects   11
Summary and Overview   13

CHAPTER 2: Concepts and Issues in Juvenile Arrest
    Research   **15**
The Three Main Approaches to Studying Juvenile Arrest   16
Correlates of Juvenile Arrest   21
Legal Variables   28
Summary   38

CHAPTER 3: Youth Gangs and Arrest   **41**
Delinquent Subculture   41
Gangs and Delinquency   44
Gangs and Arrest   45
Summary and Conclusion   48

CHAPTER 4: Modeling the Effects of Legal and
    Social Variables on Juvenile Arrest   **51**
Introduction   51
Hypotheses   52
Sample   60
Measures   62

CHAPTER 5: Testing the Race-Ethnic Labeling Hypothesis   **73**
Introduction   73
Labeling and Arrest   73
Race and Ethnic Effects in the Full Sample   78
Multivariate Modeling of the Race Effect   82
General Arrest Predictors in the Model   86
Discussion   89

CHAPTER 6: SES and the Race-Arrest Relationship   **91**
Introduction   91
Modeling   91
Results   92
Summary   99

CHAPTER 7: Gang Membership and Arrest: Specifying Race and SES Effects   **103**
Introduction   103
Descriptives   104
Gang Models   107
Summary and Conclusion   116

CHAPTER 8: Conclusion—Labeling and the Confluence of Extralegal Characteristics on Juvenile Arrest   **119**
Introduction   119
Discussion of Findings   120
Study Limitations   130
Implications for Policy and Theory   133

APPENDIX A: General Delinquency Measures, 12-Month Incidence   **137**

APPENDIX B: Delinquency By Gang Member Status   **139**

Bibliography   **141**

Index   **169**

List of Tables

Table 5.1: Self Reported Delinquency Status by
Arrested Status in the NLSY97, Waves 1 - 4 75

Table 5.2: Characteristics of "No Delinquency"
Arrestees Subsample versus the Full
Sample, Waves 1-4 77

Table 5.3: Sample Characteristics by Race: 4-year
Averages (1997-2000). 79

Table 5.4: Arrest Status by Interviewer-Rated SES
and Race 81

Table 5.5: Arrest by Race and Gang Membership 82

Table 5.6: Number of Arrests on Race and Controls 83

Table 6.1: Arrests on Race, SES, and Interactions
(n = 3,881) 93

Table 7.1: Sample Characteristics by Gang
Membership Status 105

Table 7.2: Arrests on Gang Status, Controls, and
Interactions 108

Table B.1: Four-year Delinquency Status by Four-
year Gang Member Status 139

Table B.2: Four-year Delinquency Score by Four-
year Gang Member Status 139

List of Figures

Figure 4.1: Proportion of the Sample Ever Arrested   63

Figure 4.2: Wave in Which Youth Were Arrested   64

Figure 6.1: Arrests on Race, Moderated by Income   97

Figure 6.2: Arrests on Income, Moderated by Race   98

Figure 6.3: Arrests on Income, Moderated by
Ethnicity   99

Figure 7.1: Arrests by Gang Status, Moderated by
Race   112

Figure 7.2: Arrests by Race, Moderated by Gang
Status   113

Figure 7.3: Arrests by Gang Status, Moderated by
Ethnicity   113

Figure 7.4: Arrests by Ethnicity, Moderated by
Gang Status   114

Figure 7.5: Arrests by SES, Moderated by Gang
Status   115

Figure 7.6: Arrests by Gang Membership Status,
Moderated by SES   116

CHAPTER 1:
Introduction and Theoretical Background

Expressed in the simplest terms, this is a study of race and juvenile arrest in the U.S. However, when race purports to be the central topic in a social research endeavor, the undertaking inevitably becomes multifaceted. Given its seeming inextricability from so many other social characteristics, race alone can rarely be expected to predict the outcome of interest. In fact it is often difficult to determine whether outcomes are truly attributable to race or some other characteristic that correlates with race. In conducting such a study then, one must account for the interrelatedness between race and other variables. One strong correlate of racial minority status that is relevant to the arrest topic is poverty, which in turn is linked to various other social ills like exposure to high crime contexts. Therefore, perhaps a more appropriate summation of the book's intent is to advance the knowledge on how race, social class, and delinquent subculture interact to shape arrest patterns for youth.

Crime researchers have long been interested in the impact of race and other non-legal factors on official reactions to delinquency (Black and Reiss 1970; Chambliss 1973; Gove 1975; Hindelang et al. 1981; Lundman et al. 1978; Sampson 1986; Kempf-Leonard et al. 1995). Yet, when it comes to the particular topic of arrest, the research is surprisingly sparse. Despite the arrest event being the ever-critical gateway to the justice system, studies on social risk factors are not as abundant as one might expect. In fact, since Robert Sampson's (1986) notable investigation of the effects of such variables on the outcome of police contacts with juveniles, only a handful of studies have examined arrest risk factors in this manner (Brownfield et al. 2001; Curry 2000; Hirschel et al. 2001; Hirschfield, et al. 2006; Huizinga et al. 2007; Lattimore et al. 1995; 2004; Sealock and Simpson 1998; Wordes and Bynum 1995).

While we know that black youth are arrested at a much higher rate than white youth (Puzzanchera 2009; Snyder 2008), it is not clear whether this disparity is warranted or whether police simply treat black youth differently. There are very few studies on arrests of Latino youth, thus little is known about their arrest risk and arrest deservedness in relation to that of other race-ethnic groups. Given the need to specify the conditions under which race and Latino ethnicity matter to arrest decisions, the role they play is examined here in conjunction with socioeconomic status and gang membership. Using national-level youth survey data to extend the research into these areas, this study demonstrates that racial-ethnic minority status significantly increases the risk of arrest, controlling for legal and other demographic factors. The study also shows how race interacts with socioeconomic status and gang membership status to provide a more precise depiction of the conditions under which race matters most to arrest risk.

FRAMEWORK

Although various nuances and qualifiers are noted throughout this book, there are essentially two competing perspectives on the determinants of arrest. A legal premise holds that the average patrol officer is more reactive than proactive in the execution of police duties (Black and Reiss 1970; Klinger and Bridges 1997; Lundman et al. 1978; Wilbanks 1987). Therefore, factors such as the subject's criminal history, their current offending frequency, and the severity of their crime(s) should have the strongest bearing on the chances for arrest. By this account, social groups with higher arrest rates are simply more delinquent than other groups (Hindelang et al. 1979; Thornberry et al. 2003; Wilbanks 1987), i.e. the "differential involvement" hypothesis (Piquero 2008).

Countering this argument is an extra-legal perspective, articulated in the traditions of conflict and labeling theory over the past several decades (Brownfield et al. 2001; Chambliss 1973; Curry 2000; Lemert 1951; Quinney 1970; 1974; Stinchcombe 1963; Turk 1969). It asserts that police routinely target the poor and minority groups in their patrol practices. The result is that certain groups have a higher risk for arrest, regardless of their levels of delinquent behavior i.e. the "differential selection" hypothesis (Piquero 2008). Consequently, the filtering of cases into the justice system is a biased process that unduly labels poor, minority communities and their subcultures as delinquent. This book evaluates the utility of these competing perspectives in explaining the arrest of juveniles by testing a set of hypotheses related to these principles.

LABELING AND CONFLICT THEORIES

Labeling and conflict theories are so closely aligned that it is hardly worth considering them separately. Indeed, it might be fair to call labeling a sub-theory of the broader conflict perspective (Paternoster and Iovanni 1989).

Conflict theory is concerned primarily with the idea that powerful groups take legal and other measures to maintain their dominant status in society (Quinney 1974; Bell and Lang 1985). Meanwhile, labeling theory is more genuinely focused on details in the process of disfranchising the "other" from power, via ascription. This is accomplished by assigning deviant labels to characteristics like racial minority status, poverty, and their corresponding behavioral or cultural norms.

Labeling and conflict both explain modern definitions of crime and social control in terms of class and power relations. In both perspectives, the privileged or ruling class establishes values and norms through its control of society's dominant institutions (Goode 1975). This process defines what is deviant, undesirable, and in effect, *criminal* behavior in a given historical era (Paternoster and Iovanni 1989). Certain behaviors of the poor, powerless, and marginalized segments of society are thus more likely to be criminalized than those of the elite and conventional segments of the population. Quinney (1970; 1974) has even suggested this system creates the slum conditions that it in turn deems criminal.

Tannenbaum (1938) provided a foundation for conflict and labeling in *Crime and the Community* where he wrote about criminal behavior as an outcome that is enmeshed with many routine facets of life. By his account, conflicts between diverse social groups in a rapidly changing industrial era resulted in the labeling of those with less influence as "evil" and "criminal". For example, the outlawing of once legal behaviors such as public alcohol consumption, prostitution, vagrancy, and public loitering served to regulate conduct norms in a society growing in complexity (Tannenbaum 1938: 31). Sellin (1938), too wrote of conduct norms as a set of cultural rules for comportment that were ultimately enforced by the government. In societies that allow pluralistic competition for social and cultural dominance, the most powerful groups create laws to protect their interests and customs. This power arrangement places many members of the lower class, of communities of color, and unconventional or marginalized segments of society into frequent contact with the agents of law enforcement. Because certain elements of poverty and many forms of deviance in the lower class have a public manifestation that is unsightly to the mainstream, formal control agencies are urged by the public to minimize them (Rosenthal 2000). Certain economic innovations that are common in lower class communities must operate in the "underground" market because they are condemned by the moral majority. As a result, they are formally criminalized in the legal code. In theory, the middle class, and ultimately, police patrol label the innovations of the poor as expressions of unconformity and targets them for it. In short, the hegemonic establishment criminalizes difference, especially when it exists in the context of economic poverty.

CONFLICT-BASED COMPONENTS OF LABELING

Racial and Ethnic Minorities

Race appears in several analytical frameworks under the rubric of conflict and labeling. On a macro-social level, the threat hypothesis has been used to model repressive, formal control of minority groups (Jackson 1989; Kent and Jacobs 2005; Novak and Chamlin 2011; Ruddell and Thomas 2010). On the micro-level, racial profiling and ecological contamination continue to serve as paradigms for thinking about police-minority group relations (Alpert, Dunham, and Smith, 2007; Bostaph, 2007; Vito and Walsh, 2008). In social-psychology, race-ethnic minority status is often regarded as a form of stigma (Goffman 1963; Levin and van Laar 2006), as an indicator of "subculture" (Fischer 1995), and as carrying the connotation or *label* of criminality (Mann and Zatz 1995; Martinez 2002; Russell-Brown 2009; Walker et al. 2003).

The racial profiling concept plays a role in this study's theoretical framework to account for any targeting of minorities or police saturation of minority communities while on routine patrol (e.g. Brunson and Weitzer 2009; Russell-Brown 2009). However, most often race effects on arrest are sure to be more subtle than outright profiling. Patrol officers have greater discretion over legal action on less serious crimes, for example (Ousey and Lee 2008; Engel 2005) which may provide room for harsher treatment of racial minorities. It is also important to consider typical patrol duties and how police come into contact with the public to fully assess the nature of police-juvenile relations. Patrol duties are less law-enforcement oriented than they are in providing general assistance. Arrests or citations represent only 9 to 14 percent of all contacts with the public (Bayley and Mendelsohn 1969; Reisig et al. 2004; Smith 1986). Studies of police contacts with juveniles note that most are initiated by citizen complaints or calls for service (Black and Reiss 1970; Klinger and Bridges 1997; Lundman et al.1978). The range of options police have in deciding how to deal with juvenile suspects is generally considered to be very broad. Except for one recent study showing that police in Cincinnati treat juveniles harsher than adults (Brown et al. 2009), it is widely recognized that police discretion often results in leniency for juveniles. For these types of considerations (detailed further in Chapters 2 and 4), it is best to conceptualize the effects of minority group membership on arrest as police *disposition* or *differential treatment* primarily. Race effects may also manifest as ecological contamination. Patrol officers cognitively organize the areas they patrol along the lines of race and class, and most share the belief that minority neighborhoods are generally more crime-prone (Klinger 1997; Meehan and Ponder 2002; Smith 1986; Werthman and Piliavin 1967). Police bias is thus central to this labeling perspective, as it is potentially linked to overpatrol of minority areas, differential treatment of minority subjects, and in rarer cases, outright profiling.

Social Class

In the conflict-labeling framework, the hypothesized role of poverty in elevating arrest risk is mainly based on a spatial perspective. Poverty is often characterized by several critical features that can increase arrest risk. These include substandard housing, a lack of private space, and on the extreme end, homelessness, pushing many poor subjects into public space more often than middle class subjects. Various authors throughout the years have discussed how such conditions, along with family dysfunction, drive youth to the street where they are differentially exposed to illicit markets and deviant cultural practices (Hagan and McCarthy 1992; Miller 1958; Stinchcombe 1963; Tannenbaum 1938). Since regulation of public spaces is one of the central responsibilities of patrol police (Klinger 1997; Stinchcombe 1963; Werthman and Pilliavin 1967), it increases the likelihood that lower class subjects will be processed through the justice system (Chambliss 1973;

Katz et al. 2001; Reisig et al. 2004; Smith 1986). Moreover, due process standards are lowered in the detection of illegal behavior in public spaces, resulting in easier targets for arrest than those taking place behind closed doors on private property (Rosenthal 2000). Finally, as with race, ecological contamination is salient in several studies suggesting that officers working high poverty (and presumably high crime) areas develop cynical views about its general inhabitants' crime-proneness (Klinger 1997; Meehan and Ponder 2002). Though empirical support for the effect of poverty on juvenile arrest remained weak for several decades (e.g. Black and Reiss 1970; Elliott and Ageton 1980; Hindelang et al. 1979; Short and Nye 1957; Terry 1967), contemporary literature provides stronger evidence. Studies on youth in several cities detected individual and contextual effects of poverty on arrest (Brownfield et al. 2001; Hirschfield et al. 2006; Sampson 1986; Simcha-Fagan and Schwartz 1986). In an experimental design, Ludwig and co-authors (2001) added the caveat that youth whose families relocated from high poverty to medium or low poverty areas experienced a decreased number of arrests for violent crimes, but not property crimes. Outside of the strictly juvenile context, several studies showed that social class was a strong aggregate determinant of arrest across neighborhoods (Reisig et al. 2004; Shannon 1991; Smith 1986).

In sum, theoretical and empirical insights on the use of public spaces by persons in poor areas and the ecological contamination perspective drive the expectation for a class-based effect on arrest. Poorer areas may be saturated by police patrol, and youth may receive differential treatment if they live in or "hang out" in these areas, or if they are perceived to be poor by police (Chambliss 1973; Klinger, 1997; Meehan and Ponder 2002; Sealock and Simpson 1998; Stinchcombe 1963; Werthman and Pilliavin 1967).

Gang Membership

Few social statuses are expected to increase the risk of arrest as much as gang membership. Street gangs in America represent a public enemy of sorts and they are depicted as nearly synonymous with a delinquent lifestyle in the research literature (Battin et al. 1998; Esbensen and Huizinga 1993; Gordon et al. 2004; Thornberry et al. 1993; 2003). These views are no doubt shared by police agencies, whose officers receive specific training in dealing with gangs in certain contexts. For example, a current trend in police suppression of gangs is to "arrest on sight" where civil gang injunctions are imposed, making mere membership an arrest risk (Allan 2004; Grogger 2005; Klein 2009; Maxson et al. 2005).

The distinct physical appearance cues of most gang youth and their group-oriented nature help to facilitate their targeting by police. Recognition of the signifiers of street gang subculture has become standard in police work. True to conflict theory, this has perpetuated the long held rivalry between the police and gangs (Brownfield et al. 2001; Katz and Webb 2006; Rosenthal 2000; Werthman and Piliavin 1967). Yet, we know little about the independent effect of gang membership on arrest. That is, what is the effect of mere membership in a gang on one's arrest frequency apart from one's criminal activity? Most research on gangs and arrest ignores the ratio of delinquent events to arrest incidents. Hence, there is a scarcity of tests of the labeling effect experienced by gangs, or, the effect of mere membership on arrest frequency (deservedness aside).

Although not specifically tested in a causal framework, the part of labeling theory that deals with personal identity issues is somewhat relevant to this study in that gang membership is self-reported in the data. For youth to self-identify as a gang member when asked the survey question "have you ever been or are you currently a member of a gang?" suggests something about their self-proclaimed identity. At a minimum, the youth's gang member status, or the desire to be perceived as a gang member in some cases, is strong enough for him or her to admit to real or imagined associations with a gang.

Gang membership is a deviant status on many levels, beginning with its scarcity. Where a necessary feature of a deviant status is that it is rare in the population, i.e., that it is "different" or non-conformist, it qualifies. In any given year of the survey data used in this analysis, a mere 2.5 to three percent of American youth claim gang membership.

Beyond its rareness in the population, gang membership is a deviant social status in a number of interesting ways. Even in some of the earliest theoretical notions about the conditions under which gangs emerge, youth who belong to gangs are misfits of one form or another. Cohen (1955), Cloward and Ohlin (1960), and Short and Strodtbeck (1965) each described a process by which youth who didn't perform well in mainstream institutions such as public school were ostracized and tagged as special, different, or problematic. In turn, these youth identified each other in the neighborhood and formed anti-social peer groups based on a value system that inverted middle-class values of decency and respect for society's norms.

In labeling theory, that "'attempts to do something about deviance' produce a heightened commitment to the very behavior that enforcement agents are attempting to eradicate" (Paternoster and Iovanni 1989: 362), is the quandary of the American youth gang problem (Klein 1995). Staunch allegiance to the gang and its turf have characterized the youth gang subculture for quite some time (Jackson and McBride 1996; Miller 1958; Rosenthal 2000; Sanchez-Jankowski 1991; Thrasher 1927; Valdez 2000; Vigil 1998; 2002; Werthman and Pilliavin 1967). Moreover, recent work shows that official labeling of youth significantly increases their chances of joining a gang (Bernberg et al. 2006).

That gang youth have earned their negative label by being highly delinquent is all but axiomatic. There exists, however, a strand of research claiming that differences in delinquency levels between gang and non-gang youth have been overstated (Chesney-Lind et al. 1994; Curry 2000; Curry and Spergel 1992; McCorkle and Miethe 1998; Winfrey et al. 1994; Zatz 1985; 1987). A critical test of whether gang youth are unduly targeted for arrest must control for delinquency level and observe the effects of gang membership status on the risk of arrest, net of all other legal and social variables. I employ such an analytical strategy in this study.

INTERACTION EFFECTS

In light of the various labeling principles considered above, this work seeks to determine whether race, social class, and gang membership yield independent and combined effects on arrest. To begin, each of these variables has exerted main effects on juvenile arrest in past research. There are cogent reasons to expect statistical overlap among these items as well. This nexus of race, poverty, and delinquent subculture is prominent in social disorganization theory, for example (Bursik and Grasmick 1993; Kornhauser 1978;

Sampson and Groves 1989; Shaw and McKay 1942; Veysey and Messner 1999). The notion of "multiple marginality" also depicts intersections of race, class, and gang membership (Freng and Huizinga 2007; Vigil 2002) The first interaction examined here is race × social class. When used together in prior studies, these variables present various modeling challenges. In the macro race and crime research (Land et al. 1990; McCall et al. 2010), as well as in the neighborhoods and policing research (Meehan and Ponder 2002; Reisig et al. 2004; Sealock and Simpson 1998; Smith 1986), it has been difficult to distinguish race from class effects. Moreover, their interaction has not been a significant predictor of individual-level juvenile arrest in the only other known test of this in prior research (Brownfield et al. 2001). A test for interaction is carried out here with a new design using national-level data.

A second common observation in the literature is that the youth gang population is overwhelmingly a racial-ethnic minority one (Dukes et al. 1997; Greene and Pranis 2007; Henry et al. 2001; Klein 1995; McNulty and Bellair 2003; Rosenthal 2000). This warrants a research design that accounts for such overlap. Finally, street gangs are widely known to thrive in poor neighborhoods (Curry and Spergel 1988, Dukes et al. 1997; Esbensen and Huizinga 1993; Freng and Huizinga 2007; Thornberry et al. 2003; Vigil 1988; 2002) which also warrants specification in the current study. I thus test for the interactive effect of minority status and gang member status on arrest risk, in addition to the social class × gang interaction, two tests no other study to date has executed.

SUMMARY AND OVERVIEW

The labeling propositions presented here have had some relevance to past research on justice system responses to delinquency. However, few have used them to guide research on the arrest of juveniles. This approach enables an inquiry into whether extralegal bias is present in this most critical component of the juvenile justice system that selects subjects for processing.

This work evaluates the various approaches to studying arrest risk factors for juveniles and identifies the primary conceptual issues tied to that effort. Employing a common set of correlates of juvenile arrest appearing in the delinquency literature, I offer a closer examination of the effects of several key social variables. As the social variable receiving the least amount of attention in the arrest literature, a good deal of focus is placed on gang membership in this study. Its unique role in increasing arrest risk is examined, along with its interactive role with race and social class.

This work on youths' contact with police corresponds to the latest priority of the federal juvenile justice initiative on *Disproportionate Minority Contact* (DMC). Noting the high rate of contact minority youth have with justice agencies, the initiative seeks to determine what causes DMC at various stages of involvement (OJJDP 2010b). A recent mandate calls for a focus on the earliest stages of contact, yet most research continues to study bias in the later stages of processing (Huizinga et al. 2007; Piquero 2008). The current study answers the call for research designs that account for elevated levels of minority offending in estimating any undue arrest risk experienced by these groups. Given that street gangs predominate in minority communities, they are clearly a key part of the mechanism giving rise to DMC. Similarly, that race-ethnic minorities are disproportionately poor, a significant portion of the elusive etiology of DMC is surely contained therein. The models developed for the current study were designed to help account for these layers of complexity.

CHAPTER 2:
Concepts and Issues in Juvenile Arrest Research

This chapter evaluates the three main methodological approaches used in prior studies of juvenile arrest dynamics. As this subfield becomes increasingly quantitative, the merits of survey data for such pursuits are noted. An assessment of juvenile arrest predictors appearing in the delinquency literature is also offered. With the exception of gang membership (examined separately in the Chapter Three) the current chapter provides a rationale for the set of arrest determinants chosen for the current analysis.

The first research question addressed here is whether and how being a racial minority increases the chance of arrest. Although this issue is treated rather extensively in prior research, it remains unclear why being black is often a significant predictor of arrest, net of legal and social controls. By comparison, arrest research on Hispanics is far less abundant and is virtually inconclusive. Tying these race and ethnic categories to social class and gang membership indicators in subsequent chapters offers key insights on their relationship to arrest risk.

THE THREE MAIN APPROACHES TO STUDYING JUVENILE ARREST

Prior research on the determinants of juvenile arrest essentially relies on three sources of data. Studies using official reports typically obtain them from local agencies, examining data on one or more cities at a time (e.g Bell and Lang 1985; Hirschel et al 2001), while others are national in scope (e.g. Huizinga and Elliott 1987; Pope and Snyder 2003). Use of field data on police contacts with youth provides a second approach in this area of research (e.g. Black and Reiss 1970; Brown et al. 2009; Lundman et al. 1978; Brunson and Weitzer 2009). Finally, many studies rely on self-report survey data. Several of these are national in scope (Dunford and Elliott 1984; Tapia 2010; Weiner and Willie 1971) but most are collected on youth from one or more cities (e.g. Brownfield et al. 2001; Curry 2000; Huizinga et al. 2007; Sampson 1986; Thornberry et al. 2003.) Others match official arrest data to self report data (e.g. Hirschfield et al. 2006; Sampson 1986; Simcha Fagan and Schwartz 1986), and yet others have used a mixed-method approach with official data, ride along, and interviews (Morash 1983; Wordes and Bynum 1995).

Use of official records

A large number of studies have used official data to examine arrest determinants for youth (e.g. Bell and Lang 1985; Cicourel 1976; Dannefurand Schutt 1982; Ferdinand and Luchterhand 1970; Hirschel et al. 2001; Males and McCallair 1999; McEachern and Bauzer 1967; Pope and Snyder 2003; Terry 1967; Tielmann and Landry 1981). These efforts have been informative in identifying legal determinants of arrest and potential sources of extralegal bias. However, because most delinquency goes undetected by police (Curry and Spergel 1992; Dunford and Elliott 1984; Elliott et al. 1987; Elliott and Voss 1974; Empey 1982; Farrington et al. 1996; Gould 1969; Hindelang et al. 1981; Hirschi 1969; Huizinga and Elliott 1987; Morenoff 2005; Sampson 1986; Thornberry and Krohn 2002; Williams and Gold 1972), these data may not be representative of the full distribution of juvenile offenses from which the arrests are drawn. As a small subset of all delinquent incidents, arrests may not fully capture the type and intensity of all juvenile offending (Elliott and Ageton 1980; Gould 1969; Hindelang et al. 1981; Huizinga and Elliott 1987; Ludwig et al. 2001; Snyder 2006; Williams and Gold 1972). Also, since juveniles are more likely than adults to commit crime in groups, many arrests can result from a single incident, overestimating the effect of delinquency on an individual's arrest chances (Erickson 1971; Snyder 2006; Warr 1996; 2002). Finally, agency arrest records are rife with errors in data entry, filing, and completeness (Monahan 1970). These limitations of official data make them less than ideal for a study on arrest risk. For these reasons, addressing the notion of *risk* should, at a minimum, account for the ratio of arrests to offenses committed.

Police Contacts with Youth

The police field contact method widens the universe to all youth the police encounter, but is still limited inasmuch as they are a small subset of delinquent acts carried out by the larger youth population. Many delinquent acts from the broader set would also be "eligible" for arrest, but they have failed to gain the attention of police or don't result in contact or apprehension. Much of what comes to the attention of police is based on citizen reports (Black and Reiss 1970; Klinger and Bridges 1997; Lundman et al. 1978) and may be influenced by officer characteristics, patrol area characteristics (Klinger 1997; Novak et al. 2002; Reisig et al. 2004; Shannon 1991; Smith 1986; Werthman and Piliavin 1967) or patrol directives to focus on certain types of delinquency over others (Allan 2004; Cicourel 1976; Monahan 1970). Even with police contact, most juvenile offenders do not get taken into custody. By all estimates, about 20 percent of juvenile encounters with police result in arrest (Black and Reiss 1970; Brown et al. 2009; Lundman et al. 1978; McEachern and Bauzer 1967; Myers 1999). A main reason for the low rate of arrest in juvenile-police encounters is the substantive nature of delinquent acts themselves. The vast majority of juvenile offenses are not serious or violent (Ferdinand and Luchterhand 1970; Harris 1986; Lundman et al. 1978; Piliavin and Briar 1964; Puzzanchera 2009). Therefore, officer discretion becomes extremely relevant in many juvenile cases. With the recent exception documented in Cincinnati (Brown et al. 2009), officer discretion has generally been referred to as an extension of the juvenile court philosophy of leniency and treatment over punishment, wherever possible (e.g. Bell and Lang 1985; Pilliavin and Briar 1964). Police may also be deterred from making arrests for minor incidents to avoid overwhelming the court with petty offenses which may not be successfully prosecuted (Wordes and Bynum 1995; Bayley and Mendelsohn 1969; Monahan 1970).

Finally, most studies using official and police contact data lack information on patrol area context.[1] Most police-juvenile interactions are initiated by calls for service, yet this does not account well for the roughly 30 percent of encounters that are police-initiated. The race and social class of individuals or communities may condition the targeting practices of police while in a proactive mode on patrol. This was shown in the work of Werthman and Piliavin (1967), who qualitatively focused on police interactions with minority street kids and gang youth. Theirs was largely a discussion of rivalry over public space, noting more aggressive patrols in low income neighborhoods. These authors also commented that police consider black youth to be "out of place" when seen in higher income neighborhoods, which can translate to arrest risk. Various contemporary studies of race, place, and arrest risk also depict this phenomenon (Brunson and Weitzer 2009; Meehan and Ponder 2002; Russell 1998; 2009).

Survey Data

A third source for research on determinants of juvenile arrest is survey data (Brownfield et al. 2001; Curry 2000; Elliott and Voss 1974; Hindelang et al. 1981; Hirschi 1969; Hirschfield et al. 2006; Sampson 1986; Sealock and Simpson 1998; Shannon 1991; Simcha-Fagan and Schwartz 1986; Williams and Gold 1972). The samples in survey data are typically representative of all youth in a given sampling area, delinquent and non-delinquent as well as arrested and non-arrested. Arrests are also self-reported.[2] At

---

[1] See Weiner and Willie (1971) and Sampson (1986) for rare exceptions using official data.

[2] The validity of self reported data is addressed in Chapters 4 and 5.

a minimum, these are the two components necessary for quantifying the chances of arrest. Survey data also contain a much richer set of demographic and social indicators on youth that are often absent in official or police contact data. The "no arrest" outcome in official and police contact data is essentially some form of the legal disposition of "counsel and release". In survey data, the potential reasons for being placed into a "not arrested" or "never arrested" category are more varied than in police contact data. A small portion of youth in survey data will not have committed a delinquent act during the survey period (Piquero et al. 2005) or may have avoided police detection or apprehension (Dunford and Elliott 1984). Moreover, with survey data, the results of significance tests for risk items are more reliable due to wider variability and the larger number of cases.[3]

To summarize, most early studies explored arrest risk factors with official data and observations of police-juvenile contacts. Recent efforts have shifted toward the use of survey data, in recognition of limitations of the former two data types (Hindelang et al. 1981). That is not to suggest survey data are void of limitations for studying arrest risk. They do not contain information on victim demands for arrest, the presence of witnesses and evidence, or suspect demeanor at the time of arrest, which are shown to be key legal risk factors (Black and Reiss 1970; Lundman et al. 1978; Pilliavin and Briar 1964; Reisig et al. 2004). However, survey data are free of many of biases of official arrest data and police contact data. Moreover, arrest risk factors identified in survey data typically apply to *all*

---

[3] Dannefur and Schutt (1982) provide an exception with official data.

youth with the given characteristic(s), not just to a subset of delinquency cases detected or processed by the police.

CORRELATES OF JUVENILE ARREST

Various legal and social variables emerge as correlates of juvenile arrest in the delinquency literature. The most common legal variables appearing in the youth survey research are delinquent intensity (frequency and severity) and to a lesser degree, criminal history. The ability of these legal variables to predict arrest is well-established. A rational-legal premise holds that the chances of arrest increase with offense seriousness and frequency, a view supported by studies using the three types of arrest data (Black and Reiss 1970; Brownfield et al. 2001; Dannefur and Schutt 1982; Hirschfield et al. 2006; Lundman et al. 1978; Monahan 1970; Pilliavin and Briar 1964; Sampson 1986; Simcha-Fagan and Scwhartz 1986; Thornberry et al. 2003; Williams and Gold 1972).

Although not as abundant in the juvenile arrest research as delinquent intensity, criminal history is theorized to be something of an omnibus control in the current research. It is both a legally and socially relevant control item, picking up the effects of deviant predisposition (latent traits), state dependence (environmental influences), and official labeling effects (police familiarity with youth or computerized recall of arrest history in the field). As such, it arguably accounts for much of the crime-proneness that exists in a random sample of U.S. youth (Nagin and Farrington 1992).

While a number of social variables appear in the recent survey literature on juvenile arrest (e.g. family and peer influences, difficulties in school, and mental health status), I contend that criminal history accounts for much of the influence of these items. Most studies using these social items to predict arrest fail to control for criminal history. For some, the focus has been on first-time arrest (Hirchfield et al. 2006), while for others, criminal history is viewed as more relevant in adjudicatory stages of system processing (Sampson 1986; Farrington et al. 2010). After much preliminary testing with the various social correlates listed above, criminal history appears to be a suitable global proxy for many of these environmental influences.[4] Use of this approach results in a more parsimonious empirical model for analysis. Since any race, SES, or gang-based labeling effects noted in the study must emerge beyond the criminal propensity and official labeling effect, it represents a rather rigorous test of the theory.

The effects of race and other demographic items are often explored in the arrest literature. Having received ample attention in past research, race is discussed first, followed by social class. The other demographic items covered in this review of juvenile arrest correlates are sex, age, and place (urban and rural).

Black Youth and Arrest

Historically, the black youth arrest rate is consistently much higher than that of white youth (e.g. Hirschi 1969; Snyder 2008). However, arrests of black youth appear to be too high for their self-reported delinquency level. Their self-reported serious offense rate is typically double that of whites (Elliott and Ageton 1980; Farrington et al. 1996; Hindelang et al. 1979; Morenoff 2005),[5] yet black youth are arrested for index offenses four times as often (Puzzanchera

---

[4] See Chapter 5 for additional notes.
[5] See Piquero and Brame (2008) for a recent exception.

2009), down from six times the rate through the 1990's (Farrington et al. 2003). Moreover, the racial difference in self-reported offending is not always significant (Huizinga and Elliott 1987; Maxfield et al. 2000; Piquero and Brame 2008; Williams and Gold 1972).

Researchers have offered various hypotheses over the years to explain the discrepancy between self reported offending rates and arrest rates for black youth. For some, it reflects differences in patrol of black and white communities (Farrington et al. 2003; Sampson 1986; Simcha-Fagan and Schwartz 1986). Others have considered possible differences in demeanor toward police by race (e.g. Piliavin and Briar 1964; Werthman and Piliavin 1967). Some field studies suggest that it reflects the bias of citizens, who make stronger demands for arrests of black youth than for white youth (Black and Reiss 1970; Lundman et al. 1978). Still, others have suggested that black youth underreport their delinquency in survey data (Hindelang et al. 1981), though contrary evidence has since been offered (Farrington et al. 1996; Maxfield et al. 2000).

Like many early studies on racial differences in youth offending, recent efforts of considerable sophistication also fail to tease out race effects in delinquency. For example, a handful of multilevel studies show that an individual's race loses its statistically significant relationship with violence and other serious forms of delinquency once contextual items such as neighborhood disadvantage are accounted for (Bellair and McNulty 2005; Kaufman 2005; Peeples and Loeber 1994; Sampson et al. 2005). Nonetheless, race is a significant predictor of individual-level juvenile arrest in virtually every published study in the contemporary delinquency literature that examines this issue (Brown et al. 2009; Brownfield et al. 2001; Dannefur and Schutt 1982;

Hirschfield et al. 2006; Sampson 1986; Sealock and Simpson 1998).

Latino Youth and Arrest

The growing ethnic diversity of the U.S. is not well reflected in its arrest research. In fact, much of the larger body of research on minorities and crime, delinquency, and justice is largely confined to black-white comparisons (Barela-Bloom and Unnithan 2009; Gabiddon and Greene 2009; Kaufman 2005; Martinez 2002; Russell-Brown 2009; Sissons 1979; Urbina 2007; Walker et al. 2003). The historical limitations of official and survey data have stunted research on Hispanics and crime. For example, national-level arrest data are not available for this group (Gabiddon and Greene 2009; Morenoff 2005; Sissons 1979; Urbina 2007; Walker et al. 2003).

Survey data provide a source of arrest data on Hispanic youth, but up until recently, they were not adequately sampled for results to be representative of all Latinos. They were thus dropped from the analysis in much prominent survey research (Farrington et al. 1996; Simcha-Fagan and Schwartz 1986; Wikstrom and Loeber 2000). Some of this is a function of the regions and time periods where youth studies occurred (e.g. Pittsburgh and Rochester in the late 1980's, Seattle in the late 1970's), but even national sampling frames have generally failed to capture enough Hispanic youth to analyze meaningfully (e.g. Elliott and Ageton 1980; Menard and Elliott 1990). While recent developments in survey data have helped to remedy this situation (e.g. National Longitudinal Survey of Youth 1997 and Adolescent Health), few researchers have used these data to study Latino arrest.

There is a small body of research on Hispanic involvement in the early stages of justice processing, most on specific cities, and all on juveniles. Findings from the more recent studies noticeably deviate from earlier ones in that they do find arrest penalties for Latinos. While few benchmarks exist to compare against the current study's findings, these few studies are worth summarizing, as they help to inform hypotheses for the current investigation.

Terry (1967) found that Mexican Americans were no more likely to be arrested than whites in one medium sized Midwestern city in the 1950's. McEachern and Bauzer (1967) and Cicourel (1976) also failed to observe a pattern in decisions to file petitions for Mexican, Black, and White youth in various southern California cities. By contrast, in a study of two New Jersey counties, Dannefur and Schutt (1982) found that Hispanic youth experienced a higher risk of arrest than White youth, but a lower risk than Black youth. This mid-range arrest penalty was also recently observed by Huizinga (2007) for Hispanic youth in Rochester and by Tapia (2010) using data for the nation.

In their examination of post-arrest intake decisions for youth in Los Angeles, Bell and Lang (1985) found that intake officers filed petitions for Blacks and Mexican Americans at a similar elevated rate, relative to White youth. In one recent study where race was not a main independent variable, but a control item, blacks and Hispanics were combined to yield "minority" effects (Hirschfield et al. 2006). This was done for a low number of Hispanics in the data on youth from Rochester.

Some research shows that Hispanic and other minority youth face a higher risk of arrest for curfew violations. Males and Mccallair (1999) showed that Blacks and Latinos were targeted for curfew arrests at a grossly disproportionate rate compared to white and Asian youth in Ventura, Fresno, and Santa Clara counties. Similar to the problem encountered by Hirschfield et al. (2006) only 12 Latino offenders appeared in a sample of curfew violators obtained in Charlotte, North Carolina (Hirschel et al. 2001). Like Hispanic youth in Rochester, they, too were lumped with another minority group (Asians) in the analysis.

Socio-Economic Status (SES) and Juvenile Arrest
The overrepresentation of lower SES youth in arrest data created much debate in the early literature on this topic (Black and Reiss 1970;   Chambliss 1973; Elliott and Ageton 1980; Hindelang et al. 1979; Lundman et al. 1978; Short and Nye 1957; Terry 1967; Weiner and Willie 1971). One obvious possibility is that poor youth are disproportionately involved in delinquency. However, Nye and Short's (1956) pioneering self report youth data showed that delinquency did not vary by social class, fueling the labeling perspective that the poor are unduly targeted for arrest. Labeling theorists argued that delinquency in poor areas comes under increased police scrutiny, thereby disproportionately criminalizing lower class youth (Chambliss 1973; Quinney 1974; Stinchcombe 1963).

Critics claimed that Nye and Short's self report data failed to capture serious forms of delinquency (Hindelang et al. 1979; Hirschi 1969; Monahan 1970). This was an important omission since lower SES subjects are overrepresented in arrests for more serious crimes in official data. According to Hindelang et al. (1979) the so-called discrepancy between arrest rates in official crime data and self reported delinquency rates was an illusion. They argued that if self reports measured serious forms of delinquency, the marked contrasts by race and class seen in arrest data would also emerge in self reported delinquency data. When more serious items were added to self reports, initial tests did confirm the Hindelang group's assertion, but with an interesting caveat. Race and class differences are most pronounced among high-frequency offenders (Elliott and Ageton 1980; Elliott et al. 1985).

SES Measurements and Recent Findings

Various individual and contextual measures of SES appear in the contemporary youth arrest literature. Individual-level measures include parent's education (Brownfield et al. 2001; Sampson 1986) an occupation-education index (Elliott et al. 1987; Hirschfield et al. 2006), and household poverty-level (Thornberry et al. 2003). Census information is also used to construct a variety of contextual SES indicators.

Whereas the influence of poverty on arrest remained in doubt throughout the 1960's and 1970's, the recent evidence more clearly shows a relationship. Simcha-Fagan and Schwartz (1986) were among the first to find both individual and contextual poverty effects on arrest. Sampson (1986) found only contextual effects of poverty on arrest. Ludwig et al. (2001) specified arrest relationships for violent versus property crimes. In Hirschfield et al. (2006) individual-level poverty is a significant predictor of arrest, but neighborhood-level SES is not.

Collectively, most studies report a significant effect of individual-level SES on delinquency and arrest. While some research has shown weak effects at the neighborhood level (Elliott et al. 1996; Simcha-Fagan and Schwartz 1986), others showed stronger contextual effects (Sampson 1986). To be sure, several studies combine individual and contextual SES measures (Elliott et al. 1987; Simcha-Fagan and Schwartz 1986; Weiner and Willie 1971), often with conflicting results (Hirschfield et al. 2006; Sampson 1986.) Finally, outside of the strictly juvenile context, several studies have shown that SES is a strong aggregate determinant of arrest across neighborhoods (Reisig et al. 2004; Shannon 1991; Smith 1986).

LEGAL VARIABLES

Crime Severity

As previously noted, most delinquency is not serious in nature. The most recent official data indicate that violent and serious property offenses comprise 25 percent of all juvenile arrests (Puzzanchera 2009). In police contact data collected prior to the mid-1990's spike in juvenile crime, felonies comprised even a smaller proportion of delinquent incidents, ranging from 5 to 14 percent of the total (Black and Reiss 1970; Cicourel 1976; Lundman et al. 1978). On average, these studies show that arrests were made in about 80 percent of cases where police had contact with a juvenile suspected of a serious crime. Piliavin and Briar (1964) found that juveniles suspected of serious crimes were almost invariably arrested, with the exceptions of burglary (30 percent no arrest) and auto theft (12 percent no arrest). Interestingly, however, for less serious crimes, level of severity was not a major factor in arrest decisions.

With ten years of juvenile arrest data for Philadelphia, Monahan (1970) found that 60 to 90 percent of juveniles accused of Part I Index Crimes were arrested. Of these major crimes, larceny suspects were arrested least often, from a high of 74 percent in 1957, to a low of 42 percent in 1958, and remaining low until 1968 when it rose to 58 percent. Burglary suspects were arrested in 70 to 87 percent of cases in this timeframe. These particular data show substantial fluctuation in the percent of suspects arrested over time with many nuances in crime severity by race and gender. This serves to weaken the expectation that crime severity will be such an overarching determinant of arrest.

Some have found that property and drug crimes contributed to arrest more often than violent or minor crimes, but more importantly, that social variables were better predictors than legal ones (Dannefur and Schutt 1982). Race was the absolute strongest predictor of arrest in the study and interaction effects for race by allegation were also present. Pope and Snyder (2003) also found race effects in their analysis of NIBRS (official) data – only they showed that *white* youth were six percent more likely to be arrested for violent crimes than black youth. This may speak to the nature of black youth violence as more often gang related or other street-crime related and hence more anonymous. It is also likely to reflect differentials in victim or community cooperation with police by race (Anderson 1999; Sampson and Bartusch 1998).

Overall, the rate of arrests for misdemeanors and other less serious crimes is predictably lower than for index crimes. Depending on the type of misdemeanor and race of suspect, anywhere from 4 to 60 percent were arrested in field studies (Black and Reiss 1970; Cicourel 1976; Lundman et al. 1978). In Philadelphia, Monahan (1970) found that overall, 20 to 30 percent of minor offenses result in arrest. An important caveat is that among the offenses rated as minor, gun carrying, sex offenses, arson, and receiving stolen property resulted in arrest 70 to 85 percent of the time. Arrests for incorrigibility and "protection" cases also were in the "high" range (Monahan 1970: 137).

Gambling, liquor law violations, trespassing, vandalism, and runaway resulted in arrest less than 20 percent of the time. Finally, McEachern and Bauzer (1967) made reference to the difficulty of arbitrarily coding official data on police-juvenile contacts by degree of severity. As discussed below, this is also a challenge with self report survey data.

Offense Severity in Survey Data

Since its inception in the late 1950's, the self report delinquency questionnaire has undergone much change as a data collection tool. Over time, delinquency items began to mirror the crime types in official data. Yet, even among recent surveys, the types of delinquency questions asked tend to vary rather widely. These items have been re-distributed into various types of indices in the literature, including violent, serious, street, moderate, minor, general, property, public order, and substance use, among others.

Prevalence and Incidence

All self report data yield measures of offense prevalence. That is, has the youth *ever* done the delinquent items mentioned in the survey, either in their lifetime, or in a shorter time frame, such as within the last six to 12 months. This measurement taps offense diversity (i.e. how many different types of crimes have youth committed). The individual's prevalence score may also be a sum of all items checked off, with little regard to the seriousness of those offenses. These are referred to as "variety scales" (Hindelang et al. 1981; Sweeten 2006).

While some arrest researchers do utilize prevalence measures, they are in the minority, and rightly so. Brownfield et al. (2001), for example, assessed arrest risk in part by constructing a 3-item delinquency index from lifetime prevalence of self report.[6] This yields a very limited notion of arrest risk since it fails to inform on the number of opportunities for detection. The more appropriate method of assessing arrest risk is to use incidence measures. These are frequencies or counts of delinquent acts committed, typically within the past year. The following studies have used this method.

Sampson (1986) modeled the impact of offense frequency and severity on official arrest records. For males, serious delinquency was the strongest predictor of arrest, followed by drug crimes and family/school offenses (assaulting parents, expulsion from the classroom). For females, the drug crimes index was the strongest predictor of arrest, followed by family/school offenses, then serious delinquency. In logistic regression (yes/no arrest), delinquent peers, neighborhood socioeconomic status and racial minority (black) outranked the predictive power of offense severity for males. For females, the strongest predictors were family/school delinquency and neighborhood socioeconomic status. Hirschfield et al. (2006) found that a 17-item serious delinquency index and 12 month incidence for marijuana and alcohol use reflected an increased chance for arrest, while an eight-item minor delinquency index did not.

With National Survey of Youth (NSY) data, Williams and Gold (1972) found that frequency of offending contributed to arrest risk more than offense seriousness. Most of the offenses (88 percent) resulting in arrest were detected in progress by police or citizens, suggesting that

---

[6] Have you ever assaulted someone, committed theft, or stolen a vehicle?

arrest is, to a large degree, a function of chance. One study on chronic offenders provides a profound example of this. With National Youth Survey (NYS) data, Dunford and Elliott (1984) show that of 242 self-reported chronic offenders, 86 percent were never arrested during the time of their crime spree (over a 3 year period of survey). Remarkably, 17 percent of career offenders had *never* been arrested. Over a two-year period, those youth reporting up to 100 offenses were not at high risk for arrest (about five percent were arrested). There was evidence of a tipping point, however. The probability of arrest doubled for those reporting 100-200 offenses and quadrupled for those reporting more than 200 offenses. Coupling these findings with those of Pope and Snyder (2003), it is also perhaps the case that minority delinquents are more capable at eluding the police for serious crimes, and hence have a lower rate of arrest for committing such crimes.

Criminal History

The weight given to the role of prior arrest record in this study draws on two criminological explanations of crime and arrest. Each asserts that the best predictor of criminal involvement is prior criminality, yet they arrive at that conclusion differently. By one account (state-dependence), participation in crime is the result of social conditioning, i.e. the nurture effect. It reflects reduced inhibitions and higher motivations to commit crime due to the influence of environmental cues and exposure to criminogenic contexts (Nagin and Farrington 1992; Nagin and Paternoster 1991).

The population heterogeneity explanation of enduring crime-proneness is a trait-based set of ideas that include either the effects of IQ, genetic factors, and/or early socialization practices by parents. Whatever the source, the result is a low self control "trait" that is latent, is somewhat normally distributed in the population, is a characteristic that persists over the lifespan (Gottfredson and Hirschi 1990) and that may be triggered by the environment (Nagin and Farrington 1992; Nagin and Paternoster 1991). Older studies suggest that area police tend to become familiar with prior arrestees, perhaps leading to official labeling (Monahan 1970; Werthman and Piliavin 1967). Today, patrol vehicles are equipped to conduct computerized searches of suspects' arrest histories instantaneously. By labeling theory, the cumulative effects of one's official record can result in deeper criminal embeddedness (Bernberg et al 2006; Nagin and Paternoster 1991). For these properties, use of criminal history in the model provides a rigorous test of race, SES, or gang-based labeling. In fact, its inclusion results in a rather conservative estimate of labeling effects since any extralegal effect obtained will emerge net of criminal propensity and official labeling.[7]

Ever since it was demonstrated by Terry (1963), only a small base of research shows that having a prior record is a predictor of future arrest for juveniles. Battin et al. (1998) find that a prior record with the juvenile court in Seattle by age 13 exerts a strong influence on arrest by age 15. Curry (2000) finds that youth with a prior arrest have double the arrest rate of first offenders, and in logistic regression, having a prior arrest raises the odds of arrest more than sixfold. The *number* of prior arrests also significantly

---

[7] The count-based regression models (Poisson and Negative Binomial) used here are well-suited to analyzing data that reflect such heterogeneity in the population (Lattimore et al. 2004; Long and Freese 2003).

increases the odds of arrest, but to a lesser degree. Dannefur and Schutt (1982) observed that having no prior arrests is associated with a counsel and release disposition by police.

To summarize research on the effect of legal variables on arrest chances, the risk presented by offense severity is rather intuitive, but it is not as robust a determinant as some suggest (Wilbanks 1987). In several multivariate studies, race and other non-legal variables were stronger predictors of arrest than the legal items. Factoring in offense frequency as captured in survey data adds another interesting dimension to this equation. As described by Williams and Gold (1972) and especially by Dunford and Elliott (1984), frequency of committing acts increases the odds of detection, but only past an extremely high threshold for chronic offenders, who appear adept at avoiding detection and apprehension.

Prior arrest is expected to be a strong correlate of future arrest. Some past research suggests, however, that the role of prior offenses in system processing of juveniles seems to be more important to the duties of the intake officer than to those of the officer on the street (Bell and Lang 1985; Black and Reiss 1970; McEachern and Bauzer 1967; Piliavin and Briar 1964). Yet, the studies making this claim are rather dated, conducted prior to advances in computer-based information retrieving in patrol.

Demographic Items

Sex
A well-accepted tenet of criminology is that males are the disproportionate perpetrators of crime and delinquency. Males also comprise the vast majority of arrests. However,

the gender gap in arrest has been closing for many crime categories over the past several decades (Tracy et al. 2009). This may either be due to increases in female involvement in crime or to changes in law enforcement dispositions toward female suspects. Recent evidence from several studies favors the latter explanation (Chesney-Lind 1999; Steffensmeir et al. 2005).

Literature on system treatment of juveniles has addressed whether females are afforded more leniency than males. The scope of findings on this topic is limited in at least three ways. First, much of the work is focused on later stages of justice processing (Farrington et al. 2007; Visher 1983). Secondly, studies on arrest pertain mostly to adult females or suspects of mixed ages (Novak et al. 2002; Smith and Visher 1981; Visher 1983). Finally, some work on juvenile arrest either examines only males (Hirschfield et al. 2006; Simcha-Fagan and Schwartz 1986), uses separate equations for males and females (Sampson 1986; Thornberry et al. 2003), or does not specify gender in the analysis (Brownfield et al. 2001). I briefly summarize findings of the more informative studies below.

Some have found that the risk of arrest for females is lower than for males (Elliott and Voss 1974; Monahan 1970; Williams and Gold 1972). Others have found the opposite, that controlling for offense severity and other correlates of arrest, females are more likely to be arrested (Ferdinand and Luchterhand 1970; Terry 1967; Tielman and Landry 1981). Still others have found sex to have no effect net of controls (Dannefur and Schutt 1982; Farrington et al. 2010; McEachern and Bauzer 1967).

Visher (1983) discusses the conditional role of "chivalry" in arrest. The chivalry effect is expected where male agents of the law reward females with legal leniency for performing their expected (normative) gender role. She argues that such interactions become transformed into an exchange between a man and a woman in addition to officer and suspect. DeFleur (1975) made similar observations tied to drug arrests. Some find, however, that arrest risk for males is especially pronounced in serious offenses (Monahan 1970; Sampson 1986), where one would expect a female effect since committing serious crimes is outside of the female gender norm. Of the major crimes, females are most involved in larceny (Chesney-Lind 1999; Monahan 1970; Steffensmeir et al. 2005; Tracy et al. 2009). Another key finding in the literature is that younger females are more likely to be arrested than adult females (Chesney-Lind 1978; Giallombardo 1980).

Mixed evidence in the chivalry debate makes it difficult to hypothesize about the role of gender in juvenile arrest. However, two factors help to sway expectations toward a null effect. A steady increase in the arrest of young females serves to weaken the otherwise robust feature of male offending intensity. Even if these increases are due to changes in police behavior, females' chances for arrest have increased over time.

A second consideration is data-related. According to Steffensmeier et al. (2005) a methodology that isolates the less serious forms of violence narrows the gender gap in offending. The lack of measurements for extreme violence in the current study should thus serve to narrow the gender gap in offending and further weaken the male gender effect on the chance of arrest. Although their focus is on court referrals, Farrington et al. (2010) inadvertently show no gender bias in arrest, once gang membership, gun carrying, and rebelliousness were controlled.

Age

Recent official arrest data show that with the exception of a slight drop for age 15, the proportion of youth arrested in the U.S. increases up to age 18 and beyond (Uniform Crime Report 1995-2008). A similar pattern of linear increase in arrest (with age) is also observed in the literature (Butts and Snyder 2006; Elliott et al. 1987; McEachern and Bauzer 1967; Shannon 1991; Simcha-Fagan and Schwartz 1986; Werthman and Piliavin 1967; Williams and Gold 1972). However, the same age-graded pattern is often absent in self reported *offending* (Elliott et al. 1987; Simcha-Fagan and Schwartz 1986; also see Tracy 1979). In most survey data, delinquency levels appear steady during the teen years (ages 11-17). Some have observed a peak in offending in mid-to-late adolescence (Henry et al. 2001; Williams and Gold 1972). Still, others have shown that delinquency is more pronounced in the early teen years (Thornberry et al. 2003).

Given this mixed evidence on the effect of age on delinquency, the effect of age on arrest is a key relationship to consider. That is, offending intensity is either stable or decreases with age, yet arrest risk is expected to increase with age.[8] If so, this would be a clear indication of the importance of extralegal factors to the arrest decision.

The substantive implications are that police, victims, school authorities, etc. treat younger teenage suspects with more leniency than older teen suspects. A second possibility is that such results are artifacts of the way offending intensity is measured. In this interpretation, as youth age, they may offend less frequently, but their crimes

---

[8] See Hirschfield et al. (2006) for a recent exception.

become more serious, drawing the attention of police and the community.

SUMMARY

An examination of the main approaches to studying risk factors in juvenile arrest concludes that survey data are well suited for the task. They are free of the criminal justice bias of official data and contain information on a broader base of "arrest eligible" youth. These data also enable the critical test of whether or not legal variables can fully explain the effect of race on arrests.

This review of the literature indicates that race and SES *should* be durable predictors of juvenile arrest in the presence of legal and other extralegal variables. The particular form of the relationships among race, class, and arrest are not well understood however, and certainly, least is known about Hispanic youth and arrest. Analyzing national-level data will provide a valuable contribution to the discourse on race, ethnic, and class-based dynamics in juvenile contact with the justice system.

Clearly, the most intuitive predictors of arrest are the legal factors. The frequency of delinquent acts, crime severity, and criminal history are thought to be among the more durable risk factors. It is important to note, however that survey data lack several idiosyncratic legal items shown to be key in the arrest process. Field contact data indicate that victim demands for arrest, suspect demeanor, and the presence of witnesses and evidence can affect the arrest decision (Black and Reiss 1970; Lundman et al. 1978; Pilliavin and Briar 1964). Monahan (1970) also discusses the role of public pressures to demand arrest in certain types of cases. These are also deficits of the current research, a limitation articulated in the book's final chapter.

The next chapter offers an examination of a variable that is surprisingly scarce in the juvenile arrest literature. Some would argue that in light of the "arrest on sight" edict that has strengthened police power in the current era of civil gang injunctions, that gang membership might be considered a legal variable in the arrest context. Others would argue that because the definition of "gang member" remains somewhat fleeting and ever-changing, that it is a social variable. I examine these and other issues related to relations between this group and police in Chapter 3.

CHAPTER 3:
Youth Gangs and Arrest

Of the various legal and social correlates of juvenile arrest, few have received less attention in the   than gang involvement. Given that the street gang epitomizes delinquent youth subculture, surprisingly little is known about its role in juvenile arrest. This may be due in part to the ambiguity of what constitutes a gang, or what it means for an individual to be a gang member.

This chapter explores the meaning of gang membership and more generally, delinquent subculture by considering the historical and modern conceptualizations of these terms. The limited body of research on gangs and arrest is also illustrated. The role gang membership plays in the study's labeling and arrest risk framework is then detailed. It is expected to have a direct effect on arrest odds in addition to having interactive effects with race and SES.

DELINQUENT SUBCULTURE

Among the most prominent works on the etiology of delinquent subculture was Shaw and McKay's (1942) *Delinquency in Urban Areas*, which proposed a theory of social disorganization and cultural transmission of deviant norms. These concepts were developed to explain the emergence of juvenile delinquency in urban areas, with obvious implications for youth gang formation. Rapid social change was thought to be central to this process. For example, the influx of foreign immigrants to eastern and Midwestern inner cities in the late 1800's and early 1900's created neighborhoods high in population density and poverty. These areas were also high in residential turnover and in ethnic heterogeneity, factors that disrupted social networks and the ability of the community to control crime. The problem of abandoned, orphaned, or poorly supervised and impoverished youth was largely concentrated in the cities' core and central-most periphery. Wayward youth congregated on street corners, formed delinquent groups, and eventually developed their own deviant value systems.

Delinquent groups were eventually characterized by turf boundaries and delinquent specializations such as theft and prostitution. Shaw and McKay and their contemporaries (Bursik and Grasmick 1993; Kornhauser 1978) argued that once the delinquent subculture attaches to an inner city area, it gets reproduced over successive generations, and the area becomes a breeding ground for youth gangs capable of more destructive and violent behaviors. The effect of unsupervised peer groups in increasing neighborhood delinquency is well noted even in modern disorganization research (Sampson and Groves 1989; Veysey and Messner 1999). However, it is much less clear what differentiates a delinquent peer network from a youth gang (Klein 2004; 2009; Miller 1958; Morash 1983).

The Elusive Gang Definition
Many modern gang scholars note that the precise definition of a "youth gang" or "street gang" has been debated for over a century (e.g. Ball and Spergel 1995; Esbensen et al. 2001; Howell et al. 2001). While it has become the main component of the modern connotation, the first definitions

did not include criminal activity as a necessary feature of the youth gang (Thrasher 1927). Walter Miller (1958: 14) was among the first to specify this condition, writing that the "delinquent gang is one subtype [of the street corner group], defined on the basis of frequency of participation in law violating activity." Cohen (1955), Cloward and Ohlin (1960), and Short and Strodtbeck (1965) would go on to link the formation of delinquent peer groups to the marginalization of poor youth in mainstream institutions such as public school.

The essence of the American street gang has always been shrouded in urban folklore (Jackson and McBride 1996; Klein 1995; Sanchez-Jankowski 1991; Valdez 2000). Popular representations of gang subculture are replete with initiation rites, the flashing of hand signs, brandishing of colors, use of street-based vernacular, and other cultural signifiers endowed with meaning for its members and the police. Yet, when it comes to official designations, such as the entering of gang-involved subjects into police data-bases, or in seeking aggravated criminal prosecution (Klein 2004), the identification of gang members is still not very reliable (Barrows and Huff 2009; Klein 2009).

The elusive composition of the youth gang and its membership also carries over into scientific research on the subject. For example, Dukes et al. (1997: 140) comment that "social science knowledge on youth gangs and how their members differ from non-gang youths is limited and controversial...more specifically how they differ from the general population." Morash (1983) also pointed to the difficulty in distinguishing gang formations from street corner groups both in terms of the types and levels of delinquency engaged in by each, and in features of group structure. Winfree et al. (1994) and Thompson et al. (1996)

have also found a lack of delinquent specializations for gang youth in self report data. A more recent complication in identification involves youths' attempts to disguise their gang member status from police by using conventional styles of dress, covering up tattoos, and denying their involvement (Brownfield et al. 2001; Katz et al. 2001: Katz and Webb 2006).

GANGS AND DELINQUENCY

In the quest for a concrete definition of the gang, an ongoing debate in the literature is whether frequent engagement in criminal activity is what distinguishes the gang from other subcultural groups of youth. The dominant view is that gang youth are more likely than non-gang youth to engage in delinquency (Battin et al. 1998; Bjerregaard and Lizotte 1993; Gordon et al. 2004; Henry et al. 2001). As noted by Huff (1996), most gang researchers regard the crime proneness of the youth gang as its defining characteristic. Esbensen and Huizinga (1993: 566-67) write "one point of consensus in the voluminous gang literature is the high rate of criminal activity among [its] members." Indeed, Thornberry et al. (1993; 2003) have stated that the high level of serious and violent criminality among gang members is perhaps the most robust and consistent observation in criminological research.

Estimates of the differences in delinquency between gang and non-gang youth vary widely however. Huff (1996) found the rate of offending for gang youth on most crime categories was double that of non-gang youth in Cleveland. Esbensen and Huizinga (1993) found that general delinquency rates of gang youth are three to four times higher than those of non-gang youth in Denver, and Hill et al. (2001) found the same for Seattle. Thornberry et al. (1993) found delinquency rates of gang youth to be four to five times higher than those of non-gang youth in Rochester. Finally, in a multivariate framework, many have shown that gang membership contributes to delinquency net of key controls (Battin et al. 1998; Brownfield and Thompson 2002; Gordon et al. 2004; Henry et al. 2001; McNulty and Bellair 2003; Thornberry et al. 2003).

While much serious delinquency also occurs outside the gang context (Curry 2000; Curry and Spergel 1992; Klein 1995; Morash 1983; Thompson et al. 1996; Thornberry et al. 2003; Winfree et al. 1994), findings of elevated levels of self-report delinquency by gang youth seem irrefutable. One key methodological note relevant to the current study is where Curry (2000) suggests that youth who self-report gang membership in Chicago are not as delinquent as police-identified gang youth. Thus the use of self reported gang membership in a nationally representative sample may dilute the effects of gang membership on delinquency even further than in a single city known for its high level of gang activity. Such insights, coupled with mixed quantitative findings on arrests of gang youth reviewed below might serve to rival the expectation that self-reported gang membership will significantly increase arrest risk, controlling for other legal and social variables. While a main effect of gang membership on arrest is hypothesized, it is possible that its effects will be stronger in specific contexts, such as when it is made to interact with race or SES.

GANGS AND ARREST

While gang youth would seem to invoke greater police scrutiny than non-gang youth, evidence on membership as a risk factor for arrest is extremely limited. The unique arrest risk associated with gang membership net of key legal variables like delinquency and criminal history is not well researched. Several early studies evaluated arrest data for specific cities and found little to no difference in the number and types of charges filed against gang and non-gang youth (Chesney-Lind, Rockhill, Marker, and Reyes, 1994; McCorkle and Miethe, 1998; Zatz 1985; 1987). Several recent studies purporting a link between gang membership and arrest fail to execute a rigorous test by not controlling for delinquency (Katz et al. 2001; Thornberry 2003). With no self-reported delinquency data on arrestees, the claim of "increased delinquency levels" among gang youth cannot be confirmed, and as a group, their arrest deservedness is not truly assessed.

Only three studies have provided a critical test and have obtained conflicting results. Two published articles using data from the Seattle Youth Study found that after controlling for delinquency, gang membership is not a significant risk factor for juvenile arrest (Brownfield et al. 2001; Sampson 1986). The only explanation offered for this counterintuitive finding was the low priority given to youth gangs by Seattle police at the time of data collection, 1978-79 (Brownfield et al. 2001: 79).

On the other hand, using Chicago data from 1987-88, Curry (2000) reported that self-admitted gang involvement *did* increase the odds of arrest, controlling for self-reported delinquency. With conflicting results reported for different periods in Seattle and Chicago, whether gang membership significantly increases arrest risk controlling for delin-quency is yet to be fully determined. These few studies inform the current approach, the first to provide a critical test with national-level data.

A Gang-Delinquency Caveat

As a cautionary note, there are cogent theoretical reasons *not* to expect gang membership status to directly affect arrest odds. An early description of street corner gangs suggests that because many gang boys are from disrupted or single parent households, the peer group represents more than just a friendship venue (Miller 1958). The gang may serve as an extension of the family unit and for some, even as a surrogate family of sorts. Matza's (1964) "Delinquency and Drift" perspective also suggests that youth become involved with seriously delinquent groups for reasons other than criminal motivations and opportunities. This perspective goes on to state that even the most delinquent youth have other normative roles in life, and are not particularly committed to delinquent ideals. As previously noted, some studies find no differences in patterns of offending between gang and non-gang youth in terms of their areas of "specialization" (Thompson et al. 1996; Winfree et al. 1994). Both groups largely engage in what the survey research refers to as "general" delinquency.

Field research with youth gangs also suggests that any serious offending that sets them apart from other youth represents only a small fraction of the time and energy devoted to other, non-criminal roles and activities. Moore (1978; 1992), Horowitz (1980), Hagedorn (1988), Sanchez-Jankowski (1991), Padilla (1992), Vigil (1998; 2002), Miller (2001), and Valdez et al. (2006) are among the ethnographic researchers who characterized the gang as a surrogate family, providing other needs for dejected or misfit youth. This body of research depicts the gang members' routine activities as non-criminal.

SUMMARY AND CONCLUSION

This chapter has explored the meaning, measurement, and somewhat dubious role of gang membership in increasing arrest risk independent of delinquency. Elements of delinquent subculture are seldom accounted for in research on the determinants of juvenile arrest. A brief examination of the conceptualization of delinquent subculture in the literature notes that youth gangs represent the most potent form of the delinquent peer group. Beyond that, the definition is rather amorphous.

It is clear that any research on the predisposing factors to juvenile arrest ought to include a measure of gang membership. If gang members are considered more crime-prone than non-gang youth, they should be among the most often arrested groups of youth. However, self reported gang members make up very small portions of the youth population, and a good deal of serious delinquency takes place outside the gang context, by non-gang members. An added paradox is that some police-identified and self-reported gang youth engage in minimal amounts of delinquency (Chesney-Lind et al 1994; Curry and Spergel 1992; Curry 2000).[9]

Several studies have demonstrated that arrest and gang membership are not as intimately linked as most would expect. Curry (2000), who found a relationship, also noted that the effect of self reported gang involvement on arrest had not been thoroughly studied, calling specifically for research on the effects of labeling of gang youth by police. Official labeling increases the likelihood of future arrest because the labeled youth may be suspected in neighborhood crimes, regardless of his or her actual offending

---

[9] Also see Appendix B of the current study.

intensity (Curry 2000; Werthman and Piliavin 1967). Thus, by labeling theory, gang members are under increased police scrutiny due to the widespread belief in their crime-proneness, and their chances for arrest *should* increase net of delinquency level. This is especially the case given that the data used for the current study correspond to an era in which civil gang injunctions became more widely implemented around the country, making mere membership an arrest risk (Grogger 2005; Klein 2009; Maxson et al. 2005).

This chapter noted a wide range of findings with regard to how much more delinquency gang members engage in, compared to non-gang peers. With differences in delinquency level controlled, the critical test of primary labeling effects is enabled in this study's design. Modeling how gang membership conditions the race effect and vice versa should lend more clarity to the contours of labeling in arrest. Similarly, gang membership and social class should interact in a robust manner. The insights obtained from this type of study will inform the DMC research in new ways. The next chapter states hypotheses for these and other expected relationships and provides an overview of the data and methods used to model them.

CHAPTER 4:
Modeling the Effects of Legal and Social Variables on Juvenile Arrest

INTRODUCTION

This chapter details the research design used to conduct a longitudinal study of the race-arrest relationship in a representative sample of U.S. adolescents. As the chapters proceed, the analysis becomes more refined to examine how poverty and gang membership condition this relationship. The need for such a study is driven by insufficient exploration of the race-arrest relationship in prior research. While race has emerged as a predictor of juvenile arrest in most prior studies on this topic, it is not clear under what conditions this is more or less so. The few recent studies on juvenile arrest bias typically examine the main effects of race and poverty, but not how arrest risk is enhanced or otherwise tempered by their combined effects. Even fewer studies have examined the combined effect of race and gang membership or that of gang membership and SES on arrest risk.

A series of hypotheses is offered here, specifying the expected direction and relative magnitude of each of the relationships noted above. Various labeling propositions are reflected in these statements, as informed by the review of literature in previous chapters. The following sections discuss these predictions, the sample, variables, and analytic methods used to test hypotheses.

HYPOTHESES

To establish a baseline for the study, the main effect of racial minority status in increasing arrest risk is hypothesized and tested first. This provides a basis for more refined hypotheses predicting more specific conditions under which race effects might emerge. The expected main and interactive effects of poverty and gang membership on arrest risk are further developed and formally stated in this chapter.

Race and SES

In past research on race and juvenile arrest, black youth had a higher risk of arrest than white youth, controlling for delinquency level (Brownfield et al. 2001; Dannefur and Schutt 1982; Hirschfield et al. 2006; Sampson 1986). While older studies that included Hispanic youth often found no effect for this group (Cicourel 1976; McEachern and Bauzer 1967; Terry 1967), some of the more recent studies found that they had increased chances for arrest (Bell and Lang, 1985; Dannefur and Schutt, 1982; Huizinga et al. 2007). Arguably, the social category "Hispanic" resembles "black" as a minority status variable in terms of perceived threat, stigma, and potential for police bias, thus labeling and conflict theories predict it will increase arrest risk.

H₁: Racial minority status will significantly increase arrest risk, relative to whites, controlling for demographic and legal items (delinquency and arrest history).

The relationship between poverty and arrest has been argued theoretically and supported empirically (Reisig et al. 2004; Sampson 1986; Shannon 1991; Simcha-Fagan and Schwartz 1986; Smith 1986). Insights on the aggressive use of public spaces by persons in poor areas and the ecological contamination perspective both drive the expectation that social class will explain variation in arrests. Police patrol is usually more concentrated in poorer areas and youth in those areas may receive differential treatment than those in average or high income areas (Brunson and Weitzer 2009; Klinger 1997; Meehan and Ponder 2002; Sealock and Simpson 1998; Stinchcombe 1963; Werthman and Pilliavin 1967). Therefore,

H2: SES will significantly predict arrests, controlling for race, demographic, and legal items.

Race × SES

Portions of this study devoted to modeling the conditional effects of race and SES represent the most ambitious of the objectives. While each exhibited effects on arrest and other crime-related outcomes in past research, their high level of interrelatedness was so evident in the literature that it has become increasingly difficult to justify theorizing them as independent causal forces. Yet, demonstrating the nature of their interrelatedness with any precision or clarity is rare in the crime research. Many neighborhood policing studies struggled with distinguishing race from class effects (Meehan and Ponder 2002; Reisig et al. 2004; Sealock and

Simpson 1998; Smith 1986), as did much notable macro-criminological research (Blau and Blau 1982; Land et al. 1990; Shihadeh and Steffensmeier 1996). Two groups of studies showed interesting interactions of race and social class involving both ends of the SES spectrum and the two major racial minority groups in the U.S. For black subjects, "out of place" effects emerged in studies of police behavior in higher SES contexts (Brunson and Weitzer 2009; Meehan and Ponder 2002; Russell 1998; Werthman and Pilliavin 1967). While consistent with the conflict-labeling perspective, this practice does not quite represent the disproportionate targeting of lower class minority subjects that results from aggressive patrol in disadvantaged neighborhoods, as detailed by the theories' core.

An equally nuanced, and more recently discovered interaction is that Low SES contexts provide relative insu-lation from crime in Latino neighborhoods, a phenomenon known as the "Latino Paradox" (Martinez 2002; Morenoff 2005; Nielsen, et al. 2005; Sampson et al. 2005; Sampson and Bean 2006; Velez 2006; 2009), which may have implications for the current research. Despite these caveats, the interaction hypothesis stated here is made to be consistent with the more traditional strands of conflict and labeling theory driving main effects expectations.

H₃: The interaction of minority status and Low SES will significantly increase arrest risk, relative to the effect of other SES-race combinations (Low-SES Whites, High-SES minorities).

Given the substantial theoretical and empirical coupling of minority status and poverty in the crime and delinquency literature, H_3 is an intuitive expectation. Yet, it is important to note that the only other known statistical test of the SES × race interaction effect on juvenile arrest yielded nonsignificant results (Brownfield et al. 2001). The current study has several methodological advantages over past testing however, including a longitudinal versus cross sectional design, nationally representative data versus single-city data, multiple versus single measurements of SES, and superior delinquency measures (frequencies versus prevalence).

Gang Membership

The last set of hypotheses pertains to the role of gang membership in arrest risk. Subjects who report being a current member of a gang are expected to have increased chances for arrest with race, SES, and control items in the model. This prediction is consistent with several labeling propositions. The first is the deviant nature of gang membership via its rarity in the population and its social ostracism. The widespread belief in the criminogenic nature of the gang deems it a serious social problem and a public nuisance.

A second relevant labeling proposition is linked to its recognizable social and physical attributes. Police profiling and arrest disposition may be more pronounced for gang youth, based on physical appearance cues and associations with other known gang youth (Jackson and McBride 1996; Werthman and Piliavin 1967; Valdez 2000). Also, it is difficult to identify a social group with whom the police have such an antagonistic relationship (Brownfield et al. 2001; Katz et al. 2001; Katz and Webb 2006; McMorkle and Miethe 1997; Rosenthal 2000; Werthman and Piliavin 1967; Zatz 1985; 1987).

H₄: Current gang membership will significantly increase arrest risk, controlling for race, SES, legal, and demographic variables.

Past research informs one to take a cautious approach in making this hypothesis. To begin, two of the three studies on this topic fail to find that gang membership increases the odds of arrest (Brownfield et al. 2001; Sampson 1986). However, because both of these efforts used data from the Seattle Youth Study, such replication might be regarded as a single finding. The one study that rivals this finding involved a sample of Chicago youth (Curry 2000) . It found that gang membership *did* increase the odds of arrest, beyond what can be explained by delinquency level and arrest history.

Measurement and modeling issues may limit labeling effects for gang youth. The Seattle studies referenced above use the same measurement of gang membership status as I use here. After providing youth with a definition of a "gang", they are asked to self report whether they have ever been in a gang, and if so, were they in a gang over the past year. In the spectrum of rigorous measurements of gang membership, Esbensen et al. (2001) identify this as a mid-range. This runs the risk of sampling many "wannabe" gang youth or "fringe" members that do not engage in much serious crime.[10] In terms of modeling, as the last univariate test item to enter the study, significant gang

---

[10] Assessments of gang membership that do not offer a definition of a gang before collecting the youths' report, or that do not ask about their current membership status are the least restrictive. The most restrictive measurements ask about the gang's name, its tenure, and the youth's level of involvement, i.e. whether one is a "core" or "fringe" member.

effects must be strong enough to emerge with race and SES in the model.

Race × Gang Membership

I consider the interaction effect between race and gang membership on arrest in H_5. The relationship between neighborhood racial composition and delinquent subculture has been a cornerstone of social disorganization theory for decades (e.g. Kornhauser 1978; Shaw and McKay 1942). There is also recent evidence of simultaneous effects of minority and gang status on arrest risk (Curry 2000; Curry and Spergel 1992; Thornberry et al. 2003), and qualitative depictions of an interaction effect (Rosenthal 2000; Werthman and Piliavin 1967). Given the substantial overlap of minority and gang youth categories in the delinquency literature, pairing these statuses should increase arrest risk relative to other race-gang status combinations (i.e. non-gang whites, white gang youth, and non-gang minorities).

That the youth gang population is overwhelmingly comprised of racial-ethnic minorities also compels this hypothesis. Moreover, expectations for the effects of gang membership alone are somewhat weak, reflected in the carefully qualified discussion accompanying H_4. That minority gang membership contributes to "multiple marginalization" (Freng and Huizinga 2007; Vigil 2002), also drives the expectation for various combined effects of racial minority status, poverty, and gang membership on arrest.

H_5: The interaction of minority status and gang member status will significantly increase arrest

risk, relative to other race-gang status combinations.

Gang Membership × SES

Finally, exhausting the theoretical and analytical possibilities for the study's focal variables, I consider the Gang × SES interaction on arrest frequency. While a competing hypothesis is also offered in this section, given the main effect expectations for the two items comprising the interaction, the most logical hypothesis is that gang membership will have a significantly stronger positive effect on arrest for Low versus High-SES youth. The empirical findings driving this expectation reflect that gangs are abundant in poor areas. Moreover, inner-city street corners are staging areas for gangs to claim their territory and for drug dealing, resulting in "turf battles" with police (Miller 1958; Rosenthal 2000; Werthman and Pilliavin 1967; Valdez 2000; Vigil 1988).

H_{6a}: The interaction of Low-SES and Gang member status will significantly increase arrest risk, relative to other SES-Gang status combinations (High-SES Non-Gang youth, Low-SES Non-Gang youth, and High-SES Gang youth).

Competing with this straightforward assumption are several findings on other types of Gang × SES and Race × SES interactions that help to inform an alternate, paradoxical hypothesis. In the first example, while it is well known that gang membership increases the risk of victimization (Decker and Van Winkle 1996; Peterson et al. 2004; Melde et al. 2009), one recent finding suggests the opposite scenario is common in high poverty contexts (Spano et al. 2008). This is consistent with the idea that youth join gangs for protection from certain types of threats to safety and livelihood in disadvantaged neighborhoods (Moore 1991; Patillo-McCoy 1999; Sanchez-Jankowski 1991; Vigil 1988).

A second example draws on a strand of literature evidencing "out of place" race effects. Studies show increased stops of black motorists in higher SES areas (Meehan and Ponder 2002; Russell-Brown 2009), of white youth in black neighborhoods (Brunson and Weitzer 2009), and of minority gang youth who dare to venture out of their lower class neighborhoods (Conley 1994; Rosenthal 2000; Werthman and Piliavin 1967).

Such examples extend the possibility of a paradox to the current study, whereby gang membership may protect against arrest for Low-SES youth, relative to High-SES gang involved youth. By these accounts, lower class gang youth may normally stay within their own neighborhoods to remain "in place" and minimize contact with police. Neighborhood boundaries defined by gang rivalries would contribute to this paradoxical result, where youth that are subject to attack by rival gangs will avoid venturing too far out of their immediate neighborhood.

Another potential facet of the paradox is that some gang youth are skilled at avoiding detection and apprehension by police (Dunford and Elliott 1984). Gang youth tend to know their neighborhoods well, possibly enabling them to conceal their misdeeds from police and citizens. In terms of differential association and learning theory (Akers 1998; Sutherland and Cressey 1974), gang youth are certain to learn detection avoidance techniques from peers in high-crime, high-poverty neighborhoods.

Low SES communities with dense neighbor networks may experience a "lookout" effect that decreases the arrest risk of gang youth in the area (see Browning et al. 2004; Patillo-McCoy 1999). Thus, there may be a high degree of tolerance of gang youth in lower class neighborhoods, perhaps by residents and police alike. As gang youth are considered potentially dangerous, citizens often avoid calling the police for fear of retaliation (Anderson 1999; Sampson and Bartusch 1998). Cognizant of the serious delinquency gang youth are capable of, police may be lenient toward their less-serious forms of delinquency in exchange for information, reducing their arrest frequency in the low-SES contexts where gangs predominate. An alternative hypothesis is thus offered.

H_{6b}: Gang membership will have a stronger effect on arrests for High versus Low SES youth.

SAMPLE

This research employs data from the National Longitudinal Survey of Youth 1997 cohort (NLSY97). In 1997 the Bureau of Labor Statistics took a random, multi-stage cluster sample of about 9,000 youths 12 to 16 years old as of December 31, 1996 and living in the U.S. The initial wave consists of a cross-sectional sample of respondents representative of all youths (N = 6,748) and an oversample of black and Hispanic youths (N = 2,236). These panel data contain a wide range of information collected on respondents each year, including their delinquency levels, arrests, and other legal and social indicators. Most of the information is obtained through youth self-reports with additional information gathered from the youths' parents and interviewer assessments of the youths' social environments. With the exception of items that are constant over time (race and sex), each indicator in the study is measured at each wave of analysis.

As with other longitudinal datasets, sample attrition, missing cases, and missing data are common. Follow-up interviews may be difficult to obtain for any number of reasons including death, illness, refusal to continue participation, or inability to locate (Center for Human Resource Research 2007). Overall response rates for the panels used in the current study were (N = 8,984) in 1997, (N = 8,386) in 1998, (N = 8,209) in 1999, and (N = 8,081) in 2000. Over 80 percent of youth in wave 1 are present in each follow-up.

To limit the study to juveniles, the youngest three age cohorts were selected. The youth in this sample were ages 12 to 14 at wave one, maturing to 15 to 18 years of age by the fourth wave.[11] Youth living with at least one parent-figure or guardian at the survey date and with complete data on arrests for all four waves were selected for a final person (n) of 3,881. For any missing data on independent variables for these cases, race, age, sex, family structure, geographic place, and a family routines index were used to predict values with multiple imputation in Stata. About one quarter of cases were missing on parent-reported income, with the youth's reported gang membership and alcohol use

---

[11] The reason a portion of the sample reaches age 18 in the final wave is due to differences in age at recruitment and age at interview date. While all youth were ages 12 to 16 as of December 31, 1996, they were not all that age at the actual time of interview, with similar discrepancies for each follow-up (NLSY Topical User Guide: Age of Respondent). The select statement included youth up to age 18 to keep those cases in the study.

as the next main sources of missing data, each at about 6 percent.

MEASURES

Dependent Variable

The dependent variable is the number of new arrests reported by youth in each year, averaged over four waves.[12] The use of self-reported arrest data has one main limitation. While generally considered valid (Farrington et al. 1996; Hindelang et al. 1981; Maxfield et al. 2000; Morris and Slocum 2010; Thornberry and Krohn 2002), a source of error is the ambiguous nature of arrest. This is especially true of juveniles, for whom police have the various options of counsel and release, referral to diversion, write citation, detain for questioning, and take into custody (Brown et al. 2009; Bell and Lang 1985; McEachern and Bauzer 1967; Pilliavin and Briar 1964; Wordes and Bynum 1995).

Many studies match the self-reported arrests of youth with their official arrest records for verification (e.g. Brownfield et al. 2001; Elliott and Voss 1974; Ludwig et al. 2001; Williams and Gold 1972). Since the NLSY97 does not, the dependent variable defers to contact with police perceived by subjects as an arrest. Although the vast majority of self-reported arrests show up in official records (Hindelang et al. 1981; Hirschfield et al. 2006; Hirschi 1969; Piquero and Brame 2008), it is possible for some youth to misperceive their contact with the police as an

---

[12] Allison (1990) and (Fitzmaurice et al. 2003) discuss the merits of obtaining repeated measurements of the dependent variable over time for making causal inferences.

arrest, even if officers use another, less-punitive disposition option.[13]

Figures 4.1 and 4.2 examine trends associated with the dependent variable. Figure 4.1 depicts the cumulative proportion of youth ever arrested over the four waves of the study. At well under six percent of the sample by Wave 4, arrest is a rather rare event in a population of U.S. youth.

Figure 4.1: Proportion of the Sample Ever Arrested

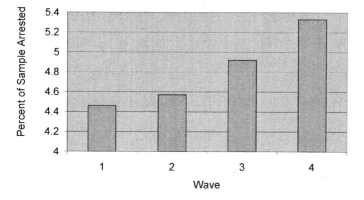

Figure 4.2 examines the trend among the arrested population. Of those arrested, relatively few experienced the event(s) in Wave 2. With this exception, arrests increased with each wave, possibly an indication of the relationship of age to arrest. That arrests across the four waves total 134 percent reflects that some youth with multiple arrests are present in several waves. The notable

---

[13] Claims of arrest in the survey lead to questions about further processing by the justice system. This cannot be used as a validity check, however, because information regarding prosecution and punitive sanctions are also self reported.

dip in arrests in Wave 2 may either reflect changes in delinquency patterns from 1997 to 1998 or in law enforcement decision-making in the U.S. in 1998, or both. For example, in a study of Philadelphia juvenile arrest data from 1955 to 1966, Monahan (1970) pointed to irregular fluctuations in the proportion arrested over time with little evidence of changing levels of delinquency.

Figure 4.2: Wave in Which Youth Were Arrested

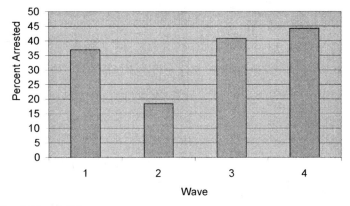

Test Variables

Race and ethnicity are represented by dummy variables for white, black, and Hispanic respondents. The "white" category is a slight misnomer in that the NLSY97's race-ethnic variable lumps all non-blacks and non-Hispanics into one category. I have labeled this group "whites" since they comprise 95.3 percent of these respondents while Native and Asian Americans comprise the remaining 4.7 percent. Moreover, Asian and Native American youth comprise a small proportion (1 percent each) of youth arrested in the U.S. (Snyder 2008). White is the omitted race category in all regression analyses. SES is measured in two ways. The first is an index derived from interviewer remarks regarding the interior and exterior of the housing unit where the youth lives, in addition to whether the interviewer feared for his or her safety. The index gauges SES from Low to High on a scale of 0 to 5 ($\alpha = .71$). It is then dummied into Low, Middle, and High SES ratings. High SES is the omitted category in regression analyses. In a separate model, I use the natural log transformation of parent-reported household income collected at Wave 1.

In the NLSY97, a gang is defined as "a group that hangs out together, wears gang colors or clothes, has set clear boundaries of its territory or turf, and protects its members and turf against other rival gangs through fighting or threats." This definition is presented before asking whether the youth has *ever* been a member his or herself. A "yes" response leads to a question about recent (current) gang membership. Current gang membership is the operational definition of "gang member" status in each wave.

Legal Variables

The antithesis to the study's labeling framework is the notion that legal variables will be the strongest and perhaps only statistically significant arrest predictors. The relevant items available in these survey data are the subject's frequency of offending, crime severity, and criminal history. Youth self-report the number of delinquent acts over the past 12 months, ranging in severity from theft to

assault with injury.[14] Such incidence measures are well-suited to estimating arrest risk since the chances of arrest should increase with the frequency of illegal behavior. Controlling for these items accounts for the differential involvement of minority and gang youth in delinquency.
Minor Delinquency. Substance use items and vandalism are grouped as minor delinquency. Alcohol use is measured as the number of occasions in the last 30 days in which five or more alcoholic drinks were consumed. Marijuana use measures the number of days respondents used the substance over the past month. The number of times the respondent used cocaine or other hard drugs in the past year is also included. Vandalism is the reported number of times youth vandalized or destroyed property in the past year.
Serious Delinquency. Assault, the property crime index, and drug sales are grouped as serious delinquency. Assault is the reported number of times youth assaulted or caused bodily injury to others since the last wave. Property Crime is an incidence composite of several theft items and handling stolen property, with scores ranging from 0 to 13 (α = .62). Involvement in drug sales is also an annual frequency measure.
Recode and Weighting. A common criticism of incidence-based delinquency measures is that undue weight is given to minor and high frequency offending, negating true interval properties (Sweeten et al. 2009). The difference between 0 and 1 assaults is not the same as the difference between 10 and 11 assaults, for example, nor is 1

---

[14] The strongest correlations registered between delinquency items were for the property crime index and vandalism (r = .47), and for selling drugs and marijuana use (r = .40). No other correlations were in this range. STATA diagnostics detected no collinearity issues among the set of variables in the study.

assault comparable to 1 act of minor vandalism. The recode procedure (see Appendix A) imposes semi-arbitrary weights to capture the seriousness of each type of delinquency, as informed by the literature. For example, in serious forms of delinquency, only the high frequency values are collapsed, indicating it is a serious enough act to warrant an arrest if detected by police or that it is a common type of juvenile arrest (Puzzanchera 2009). Collapsing more categories reflects that they have a low detection rate (as in the case of drug dealing) or are less likely to warrant an arrest if detected, due to low citizen report and more police discretion, as in the case of minor property crime.

This type of adjustment also addresses respondent exaggeration (Elliott et al. 1987; Maxfield et al. 2000). Extremely high values may be careless estimates based on youths' inability or unwillingness to recall the number of incidents. For example, Thornberry and Krohn (2002) have noted "testing effects" as responses given haphazardly to advance to the next question in the event of a lengthy interview. Extremely high counts on delinquency items are outliers with poor face validity, and thus assigned to the highest value in the recode, thereby reducing skewness in their distributions (See Matthews and Agnew 2008).[15]

---

[15] While some chronic offenders may truthfully report a high number of offenses, at least one empirical consideration serves to minimize its importance to arrest risk. The relationship of offending frequency to arrest may be curvilinear. Dunford and Elliot (1984) provide one of the few forays into this issue, noting that delinquent incidence has little effect on arrest risk after a certain threshold. Some chronic offenders appear adept at avoiding detection for their misdeeds, thus delinquent frequency matters less for them after a certain point. The coding for the current study accounts for both frequency and seriousness of offending, but imposes a threshold of about 10 offenses for most forms of delinquency. Higher counts are assigned the "ceiling" weight since they

Criminal History. Prior record is a running total of the arrests accumulated up to each wave prior to the current year's arrests (i.e. the dependent variable), in the form of $Y_2 - Y_1$, and into later waves, $Y_4 - (\Sigma Y_i)$.[16] In Wave 1, prior arrests is Y_0, capturing the total number of pre-survey arrests. In their contacts with youth, police will normally be able to obtain an arrest history. Prior arrests should result in an increased willingness to make a new arrest i.e. "official labeling" (Curry 2000; Monahan 1970; Werthman and Piliavin 1967). This, in turn, can result in a secondary labeling effect where after repeated arrests, the youth internalizes the identity of "lawbreaker" (Bernberg et al. 2006; Nagin and Paternoster 1991) .

Control Variables

Like the test items, the group of demographic control items used here has explained variance in juvenile justice outcomes in past research. Yet, with sparse research on the determinants of juvenile arrest in the last few decades, there is not much consensus on their expected effect. Holding them constant not only helps to isolate labeling effects on key extralegal variables for evaluation of hypotheses, but offers a reevaluation of the effect of these demographic items themselves on juvenile arrests.

Sex is a dummy variable equal to "1" for males. Because males engage in more serious delinquency than females (Elliott et al. 1987), are more often involved in gang activity (Dukes et al. 1997; Esbensen and Huizinga 1993), and because they comprise the vast majority of

---

are thought to be of little consequence to an already-elevated arrest risk.

[16] Prior arrests correlate with current year arrests at .30.

juvenile arrests in the U.S. (Puzzanchera 2009), I control for sex. This helps to avoid confounding the effects of delinquency or gang membership on arrests with an unobserved male effect. Controlling for sex also addresses long held debates about the closing of the gender gap in juvenile arrests (Chesney-Lind 1999; Steffensmeir et al. 2005; Tracy et al. 2009), and the positive male effect on juvenile arrest (Elliott and Voss 1974; Monahan 1970; Williams and Gold 1972) versus the positive female effect (Ferdinand and Luchterhand 1970; Terry 1967; Tielman and Landry 1981).

Age is a continuous variable, from 12 to 18. Two factors make it a critical demographic control to include in these models. First, there is some uncertainty about the effect of age on arrest, and virtually no research that examines its effect in a longitudinal design. A positive effect is frequently observed in the literature.[17] Yet, this positive effect of age is often absent in self reported delinquency, posing a contradiction of sorts. Secondly, because the odds of having accrued a juvenile record are partly a function of age (younger teens less likely to have had a chance to accumulate an arrest record) it is important to measure these processes separately.

Geographic place is a dummy variable equal to "1" for urban location, based on respondent addresses in ArcView (NLSY97 Topical Guide: Geographic Indicators 2009). Self reported adolescent violence and official arrest rates for juvenile violence are higher in urban versus non-urban contexts (McNulty and Bellair 2003; Osgood and Chambers 2003). Also, while there is growing evidence of the spread of gang formations to rural areas (Evans et al.

---

[17] See Hirschield et al. (2006) for a recent exception.

1999; Weisheit and Wells 2004), it is a long-held assumption that gang activity predominates in urban areas (Klein 1995; Miller 1958; Padilla 1992; Rosenthal 2000; Sanchez-Jankowski 1991; Short 1965; Vigil 1988). Finally, Laub (1981) has shown that less-serious crime (comprising most incidences of juvenile delinquency) is reported more often in rural settings than in urban ones.

Analytic Method

I begin making the empirical case for labeling with descriptive statistics on a pool of potentially "bad" or seemingly legally unfounded arrests. Advancing to the full sample, means comparisons by race are made for arrest and all other items in the analysis. Contingency tables then explore the relationships between race, SES, and gang membership. In the multivariate arena, Random Effects regression procedures for low-count data (i.e. arrests) are used to evaluate six hypotheses over three chapters.

Statistical Modeling

The inclusion of race and sex, both stable characteristics, precludes the use of fixed effects, warranting a random effects model (REM) (Wooldridge 2002). The main advantage of REM in a repeated-observation design is the error term is uncorrelated across subjects. In addition, unlike fixed effects models, findings from random effects analyses enable inferences about (arrest dynamics in) the larger population from which the sample is drawn, U.S. adolescents in this case.

Counts with many zero values and with no theoretical upper limit (e.g. number of arrests) are well suited to analysis with either Poisson or Negative Binomial regression procedures. Although Poisson can yield inefficient estimates when the variance exceeds the mean on the outcome variable[18], or in the case of serial dependence[19] (Cameron and Trivedi 1998; Long and Freese 2003), it has been noted elsewhere that *random effects* Poisson models, in particular, can account for overdispersion and serial dependence in the data Wooldridge (2002: 672). This appeared to be the case with several of the gang models, where Poisson provided the best fit to the data based on pseudo r-squared and where dispersion diagnostic criteria were not very compelling.[20] Negative Binomial regression was chosen for most analyses based on these same criteria.[21]

With all time-varying items measured at each of the four waves, random effects regression coefficients reflect the average effect of predictors on the average number of arrests (Fitzmaurice et al. 2003). The case ID serves to average the values for each case across waves but stacks person-period units, quadrupling the (n) of observations. This model was chosen over one that clusters the cases by

---

[18] Arrest descriptives in Table 5.3 of Chapter 5 indicate that these observations are overdispersed, with a variance-mean ratio of 2.6, confirmed in the Likelihood Ratio test of the race regression model (Table 5.4); Chi-sq = 1003.89, p<.0000.

[19] As detailed in Chapter 2, having a prior arrest is a predictor of future arrests, a possible violation of the assumption of independence of observations.

[20] Likelihood ratio test for overdispersion where the H_0 that alpha = 0 was rejected by a slim margin.

[21] Fortunately, in practice, there is not much difference in results between the models. With a few exceptions on individual delinquency items, significance results are consistent and slope size for arrest predictors is often comparable between the two count models. In the case of criminal history, however, there is a marked difference in the size of the slope. The effect obtained with Negative Binomial is considerably larger than the size of the effect obtained with Poisson.

ID to analyze within-individual changes on arrest risk (ideally studied with fixed effects). Rather, I analyze between group differences by gang membership status and SES (both subject to change) and racial minority status, a constant.

Approach

The analytical strategy most common to the literature on detecting racial bias in the juvenile justice system is the use of reduced form equations, entered in hierarchical fashion to note whether the race effect can be explained by other factors (Huizinga et al 2007). I use this approach in the multivariate analysis in Chapter 5 by first examining a baseline equation of race and demographic controls, then entering minor delinquency, serious delinquency, and finally criminal history. The ability of the race items to register positive, significant regression coefficients in the presence of these legal items is a direct test of H_1.

From this baseline, Chapter 6 evaluates the main and conditioning roles of SES on arrest risk in tests of H_2 and H_3. Tests are conducted with both the perceptual and income-based SES measures described above. Chapter 7 examines the main and conditioning roles of gang membership in tests of H_4, H_5, and H_6. Significant interactions in Chapters 6 and 7 are probed for clearer interpretation of effects.

CHAPTER 5

Testing the Race-Ethnic Labeling Hypothesis

INTRODUCTION

While the research examining the effect of race in juvenile justice outcomes is substantial, a disproportionately small amount of it is done on arrest. Most investigations into this issue have found that black and Hispanic youth stand a higher risk of arrest than do white youth. The current research improves upon past efforts by revisiting the question with national-level data and by interacting race with other social variables to specify its role in arrest dynamics. This chapter offers an empirical justification for the labeling perspective, presenting descriptive and multivariate analyses, prior to further probing with interaction effects in Chapters 6 and 7.

LABELING AND ARREST

Like many social science theories, labeling exists on a continuum of moderate and extreme perspectives. Labeling purists would argue that certain groups have increased susceptibility to criminal justice processing, based on skin-color, socioeconomic status, and other social characteristics. Taking the extreme labeling position on juvenile arrest processes is to argue that police routinely target the poor and minority youth in their patrol practices, or at least that they treat them differently in their encounters. These groups are thus expected to have a higher risk for arrest, regardless of their levels of delinquent behavior.

A moderate position recognizes the growing professionalism in policing and adherence to the justice ideal that is becoming more codified among law enforcement agencies nationally, often with the expressed goal of eradicating racial profiling. Most legal scholars and perhaps even moderate labeling theorists might more readily assume that people are arrested primarily on the basis of committing illegal acts. All other considerations or biases affecting the arrest decision would be secondary, at best.

It follows that non-offenders are not truly arrest eligible. Barring any anomalies such as mistaken identity or other errors in police investigation leading to false arrest, non-offenders would not be arrested. Then perhaps the most compelling case for labeling is to show that 1.) some youth can be arrested for no apparent legal reason; and 2.) these youth are disproportionately race-ethnic minorities, members of the lower class, gang members, or "all of the above." I begin with this premise to explore the extent to which there is a basis for labeling theory in the current research context using descriptive information on various components of the sample. Table 5.1 examines the four-year self reported delinquency status[22] by four-year arrest status for the full sample.

---

[22] For the delinquency items included in this study only.

Table 5.1: Self Reported Delinquency Status by Arrested Status in the NLSY97, Waves 1 - 4

Delinquency	Arrested	
	No	Yes
No	8,952	131
	(65.3%)	(19.6%)
Yes	4,747	538
	(34.7%)	(80.4%)

(n) of person-period observations (4 years) = 14,368. Missing cases stem from the use of non-imputed delinquency variables.

Nearly 20 percent of youth who self reported an arrest over the four waves reported engaging in none of the various types of delinquent acts examined in this study. Such a high figure may be due to the somewhat restricted range of "actionable" (Thornberry et al. 2003) or "arrestable" offenses examined. As previously described, these include alcohol and drug use, vandalism, petty and grand theft, handling stolen property, assault, and selling drugs.[23] It is from these 20 percent of arrests with no apparent delinquency that one can roughly deduce the proportion of legally unfounded arrests.

The delinquent acts examined in the current study are often referred to as "general delinquency" items in the literature (Hindelang et al. 1981; Thornberry and Krohn 2002). Status offenses such as runaway or curfew violations were not included in the study because many municipalities and other places in the U.S. do not typically arrest for these

---

[23] It is unknown whether youth would include acts of arson in the NLSY97's vandalism question asking "Have you ever purposely damaged or destroyed property that did not belong to you?"

actions, but handle them informally.[24] On the other end of the offending spectrum, certain serious crimes such as murder, rape, or other sex crimes are not available in the data. Altogether, these unmeasured crime types account for about 15 percent of all juvenile arrests in the U.S. in the late 1990's when these data were collected (Snyder 1999). This still leaves a sizeable portion of the 20 percent of arrests unaccounted for by any form of delinquency. In other words, perhaps about ¾ of these 131 arrest cases could be arrests for offenses not included in the study, suggesting that about five percent of all juvenile arrests are made for reasons other than delinquent activity. These are possibly "bad arrests", and ultimately, a pool of potential cases for wrongful adjudication (Huff 2002).

Another slight possibility is that some portion of these 131 youth is not being truthful about their arrests or their delinquency. It is important to recall however, that after much scrutiny over years of research, self report crime measurements for youth are deemed surprisingly valid (Elliott and Ageton 1980; Elliott et al. 1987; Farrington et al. 1996; Hindelang et al. 1981; Maxfield et al. 2000; Raskin-White et al. 2002; Thornberry and Krohn 2002). As noted in Chapter 4, when studies have the ability to cross-check, most self reported arrests show up in official records (Hindelang et al. 1981; Hirschfield et al. 2006; Hirschi 1969; Piquero and Brame 2008). Unable to cross-check arrest data for the NLSY97, this research must rely on the validity track record of self report youth data. Table 5.2 examines the characteristics of these youth who claim to

---

[24] The Juvenile Justice and Delinquency Prevention Acts of 1974 and 1992 strongly discourage formal processing of status offenses.

have been arrested without committing any of the forms of delinquency examined in this study.

Table 5.2: Characteristics of "No Delinquency" Arrestees Subsample versus the Full Sample, Waves 1-4

	N	Subsample (n) = 131 Mean [a] (SD)	Full Sample (n) = 3,881 Mean [a] (SD)
Race			
White	49	.37^^ (.48)	.54 (.50)
Black	38	.29^[b] (.45)	.24 (.43)
Hispanic	44	.34[b] (.47)	.21 (.41)
SES (n=118)[c] *Interviewer Rating*			
Low SES	19	.16[d] (.37)	.07 (.25)
Mid SES	60	.51[e] (.50)	.42 (.47)
High SES	39	.33^^ (.47)	.51 (.48)
Wealth			
Gross HH Income . (in thousands)	99[c]	$32.5^^^ (28.5)	$46.6 (37.2)
Gang Membership (n= 124)[c]	6	.048 (.21)	.020 (.14)

[a]   Means are four-year averages.

^   Significantly different from Full sample mean at p < .10, ^^ p < .05, ^^^ p < .001 in a 2 sample t-test

[b]   Significantly different from White mean at p < .001

[c]   Reflects missing data.

[d]   Significantly different from High SES at p < .10.

[e]   Significantly different from High SES at p < .15.

Table 5.2 shows that a smaller proportion of the "non-delinquent", arrested subsample of youth is white, as compared to the proportion of whites in the total sample and as compared to blacks within the subsample, both statistically significant relationships. Hispanics are overrepresented in the labeling subsample as well, providing preliminary evidence of disproportionate arrests of minority youth with the possibility of weak justification or no legal cause.

Interviewer-generated SES ratings and parent-generated SES measurements offer different vantage points on the class composition of the labeling Subsample. By rated SES, it is mostly comprised of Mid SES youth and least comprised of Low SES youth. The proportion of High SES youth in the Subsample is significantly larger than the proportion of Low SES youth. With Income as SES, however, the labeling Subsample is of a significantly lower SES than the Full Sample (right hand column).

Finally, gang youth are overrepresented in the labeling subsample. They account for nearly five percent of arrested youth with no self-reported delinquency, but only two percent of the full sample. However, because the number of gang youth in the subsample is small (n) = 6, the relationship is not significant. While not the most compelling demonstration, it is enough to raise some concern about the potential for differential treatment of the test groups in a particular arrest context.

RACE AND ETHNIC EFFECTS IN THE FULL SAMPLE

Table 5.3 provides the starting point to addressing the race-arrest question in the full sample. It shows that the mean arrest figures of minority youth are significantly higher than those of whites. Having established this difference on arrest, means comparisons for all other variables by race follow.

Table 5.3: Sample Characteristics by Race: 4-year Averages (1997-2000).

	White n = 2,094		Black n = 960		Hispanic n = 827	
	Mean	s.d.	Mean	s.d.	Mean	s.d.
Arrested	.04	.20	.05**	.23	.05*	.22
Arrests	.068	.40	.096**	.53	.088*	.52
DEMOGRAPHIC						
Male	.53	.50	^.49**	.50	.51	.50
Age	15.19	1.60	15.27**	1.61	15.20	1.61
Urban	.29	.45	.51**	.50	.51**	.50
LEGAL						
Minor Delinquency						
Alcohol Use	.93	2.97	^.43**	2.09	^.76**	2.63
Marijuana Use	1.04	.05	^.70**	.06	^.86**	.07
Hard Drug Use	3.95	.59	3.15	.66	3.44	.96
Vandalism	.29	.95	^.18**	.74	.26	.95
Serious Delinquency						
Assault	.20	.88	.31**	1.07	.25**	.99
Property Crime Index	.31	1.15	^.22**	.97	.29	1.15
Drug Sales	.09	.51	^.03**	.27	^.07**	.39
Criminal History						
Prior Arrests	.11	.64	.15**	.72	.15**	.81
SES						
Interviewer Rating						
Low	.04	.20	.13**	.32	.09**	.27
Mid	.35	.46	.51**	.48	.49**	.48
High	.61	.47	^.36**	.46	^.42**	.47
Wealth						
Gross HH Income (in thousands)	$59.7	41.3	^$28.4**	22.6	^$33.7**	23.1

* Significantly different from the white mean at p < .05, ** p < .01 in a 2 sample t-test with equal variances.
^ t-value for group is negative

Consistent with prior research on U.S. youth, compared to whites, both minority groups are more likely to live in urban versus non-urban areas (McNulty and Bellair 2003) and to live in lower and middle, versus high SES contexts (Farrington et al. 2003; Kaufman 2005; McNulty and Bellair 2003; Peeples and Loeber 1994; Wikstrom and Loeber 2000). The well-documented penchant for substance use among white youth is evident here (see review in Watt and Rogers 2007). Other familiar insights from the delinquency literature are minority youth engage in more assaultive behaviors (Farrington et al. 2003; McNulty and Bellair 2003), and accumulate lengthier criminal records (Curry 2000; Huizinga and Elliott 1987). That property crime and drug sales are markedly higher among whites than minorities adds an interesting footnote to the debate on the differential involvement of minority youth in delinquency. While official rates of arrest of minority youth for these crime types are higher than for white youth (Snyder 1999), the latter report engaging in more of this activity.

SES and gang membership help to clarify the role of race in arrest dynamics throughout the study. To begin exploring these patterns, Tables 5.4 and 5.5 tabulate race and arrest by SES and gang status.

The SES-race arrest relationships in Table 5.4 are very weak, as seen in the Cramer's V statistic, which ranges from 0 to 1. The only significantly specified race-arrest relationship exists in the High SES category. Blacks are the most arrested race group among High SES subjects, followed by Hispanics. This might be consistent with notions that minority youth appear "out of place" in higher SES contexts, leading to elevated arrests of those subjects. This is one of several outcomes explored further with multivariate modeling in Chapter 6.

Table 5.4: Arrest Status by Interviewer-Rated SES and Race

	White n (%)	Black n (%)	Hisp n (%)
Low SES			
Arrested	45 (11.2)	35 (8.3)	25 (10.4)
No arrest	358 (88.8)	384 (91.7)	215 (89.6)
Total (n)	403	419	240
Chi-sq		3.3	
Cramer's V		.07	
Mid SES			
Arrested	153 (6.0)	106 (6.2)	85 (5.8)
No arrest	2,378 (94.0)	1,608 (93.8)	1,383 (94.2)
Total (n)	2,531	1,714	1,468
Chi-sq		2.1	
Cramer's V		.03	
High SES			
Arrested	160 (3.2)	57 (4.1)	56 (3.7)
No arrest	4,900 (96.8)	1,339 (95.9)	1,435 (96.3)
Total (n)	5,060	1,396	1,491
Chi-sq		7.0*	
Cramer's V		.04	

* $p < .05$

Table 5.5 shows that the most arrested race group among gang youth are Hispanics. The proportion of arrested gang members who are Hispanic is seven percent higher than that for whites or blacks. Among non-gang arrestees, blacks are slightly overrepresented. Neither of these relationships is significant however.

Table 5.5: Arrest by Race and Gang Membership

	Gang Member			Non-Gang		
	White	Black	Hisp	White	Black	Hisp
	n (%)	n (%)	n (%)	n (%)	n (%)	n (%)
Arrested	25	22	34	305	158	120
	(24.5)	(24.7)	(31.7)	(3.8)	(4.5)	(3.9)
No arrest	77	67	73	7721	3313	2937
	(75.5)	(75.3)	(68.3)	(96.2)	(95.5)	(96.1)
Total (n)	102	89	107	8026	3471	3057
Chi-Squared	1.7			4.6		
Cramer's V	.09			.02		

Overall, descriptive statistics begin to make a case for labeling, suggesting that race is related to the risk of arrest, and it may be conditioned by class and gang status. However, these results are not totally consistent nor do they present very strong evidence and hence the form of the race-arrest link is still rather vague. Regression models in the next section and in subsequent chapters help to clarify this link with a full set of controls and rigorous tests of hypotheses.

MULTIVARIATE MODELING OF THE RACE EFFECT

With some preliminary support for the notion that race-ethnic minority status is related to the risk of arrest, the regression analysis in Table 5.6 tests the durability of that relationship in the presence of demographic and legal controls. Reduced form equations in Table 5.6 are entered in successive blocks to note changes in the initial effect. A baseline equation of race and demographic controls is examined in Column 1, followed by the various legal item blocks, entered successively in the remaining columns. This is a direct test of the hypothesis that race is a significant predictor of arrest.

Table 5.6: Number of Arrests on Race and Controls

	B (SE)			
	1 Race and Demog. Controls	2 Minor Delinq.	3 Serious Delinq.	4 Criminal History
RACE				
White	–	–	–	–
Black	.287***	.696***	.579***	.465***
	(.105)	(.118)	(.118)	(.120)
Hispanic	.189*	.465***	.459***	.284**
	(.109)	(.124)	(.123)	(.128)
DEMOGRAPHIC				
Male	.995***	.922***	.944***	.742***
	(.091)	(.103)	(.103)	(.0105)
Age	.105***	.066**	.052	-.038 (.033)
	(.028)	(.033)	(.033)	
Urban	.312***	.107 (.104)	.094	.040
	(.093)		(.104)	(.107)
LEGAL				
Minor delinquency				
Alcohol use	–	.100***	.091***	.051***
		(.015)	(.015)	(.011)
Marijuana use	–	.060***	.035***	.028***
		(.009)	(.009)	(.009)
Hard drug use	–	.000	.001	.001
		(.001)	(.001)	(.001)
Vandalism	–	.360***	.058 (.052)	.054 (.049)
		(.043)		

Table 5.6, Number of Arrests on Race and Controls (continued)

	B (SE)			
	1 Race and Demog. Controls	2 Minor Delinq.	3 Serious Delinq.	4 Criminal History
Serious delinquency				
Assault	–	–	.274*** (.041)	.213*** (.037)
Property crime	–	–	.231*** (.040)	.223*** (.036)
Drug sales	–	–	.067 (.088)	.061 (.084)
Criminal history				
Prior arrests	–	–	–	1.12*** (.080)
Pseudo r-squared	.02	.07	.09	.15

* $p \leq .10$ ** $p \leq .05$ *** $p \leq .01$

Column 1 establishes that race has an effect on arrest, net of demographic items. Findings support a labeling hypothesis if race items remain significant past the entry of legal items through Column 4. In Column 2, race effects were strengthened substantially with entry of the less serious forms of delinquency. In light of the principle that less-serious forms of delinquency allow for considerable police discretion in making the arrest decision (Black and Reiss 1970; Engel 2005; Lundman et al. 1978; Ousey and Lee 2008; Piquero 2008) this is a key finding. This type of discretion seems to increase arrest risk for minority youth. To be sure, the model's r-squared continued to increase when serious delinquency was entered in the next equation, while race effects were somewhat weakened. This suggests that officers were more prone to make arrests for serious offenses, with little regard for the suspect's race. On less serious crimes allowing for police discretion however, officers were more punitive toward minority youth. The race indicators remained significant past the entry of serious delinquency in Column 3 and criminal history in Column 4, offering clear and convincing support for H_1. Consistent with past research, minority status increased the risk of arrest, even after controlling for key demographic and legal items. One point of note is the black slope was larger than the Hispanic slope. Black racial status increased the expected number of arrests by about 0.46 versus 0.28 for Hispanics.[25] The black slope never dropped in its level of significance, while the Hispanic slope was slightly weakened with the entry of criminal history. Some have also found a mid-range level of bias against Hispanic youth relative to whites and blacks (Dannefur and Schutt 1982), while others found equal levels of bias against blacks and Mexican Americans (Bell and Lang 1985).

Addressing the remaining objectives of this research requires more specific delineation of race effects on arrests of youth. However, at this point, it is worth noting that the support found for H_1 has implications for labeling theory and for recent federal policy requiring states to address disproportionate minority contact (DMC) with the juvenile justice system. This demonstration of the positive main effect of racial minority status on arrest net of relevant controls cogently suggests the labeling of juveniles occurs on a national scale. Whereas analyzing data on a representative sample of U.S. Latino youth has been absent in past research (Walker et al. 2004) these findings break

---

[25]. Count model coefficients are expressed as a natural logarithm (Cameron and Trivedi, 1998; Long, 1997; Long and Freese, 2003; Wooldridge, 2002).

new ground in that arena. The drawback to using such a broad sample is that it masks the patterns in particular states and in other locales where problems of DMC are more or less severe, if at all present. A benefit of the national scope of the study however, is the increased reliability in gauging the effects of general arrest predictors in survey data.

GENERAL ARREST PREDICTORS IN THE MODEL

Several interesting results emerge from demographic and legal item coefficients in Table 5.6. Contrary to the expectation that sex would not play a significant role in arrests, male status is a significant predictor. While this is consistent with some past research, several factors caused me to expect no sex effect. This includes recent evidence of a rather rapid closing of the sex arrest gap, evidence of no sex effect and evidence that females are arrested more often after controlling for offense severity.

Much prior research finds that arrest increases with age. However, results in the current study are more consistent with recent evidence of no age effect on arrest in youth survey data (Hirschfield et al. 2006). Future work should continue to examine the age effect for several reasons. First, of the many studies finding age effects, few employ longitudinal designs. Shannon's (1991) research uses panel data, but only on youth from a single mid-sized city. Hirschfield et al. (2006) use data with the same limitation, and also take only a single measurement of age (at Time I). Moreover, their research focus is on first time arrest, where the age effect is explained by several mental health factors. The current juvenile arrest study appears to be the first to use national data with repeated age measurements for the same individuals over time. Here, the age effect is sustained past the entry of minor delinquency items, but is ultimately explained by serious delinquency and criminal history. This latter result may be due to the inherent link between age and prior arrests, where prior arrests are partly a function of age. Their zero order correlation is .12. Consistent with past research, alcohol use is a repeatedly significant arrest predictor. Although the effect is weak, it is an intuitive finding since alcohol use is widely known to create behavioral changes conducive to arrest such as aggression, risk taking, and reduced self awareness. (Raskin-White et al. 2002). Other inherent risks alcohol use brings for arrests of youth are offenses involving underage consumption, public intoxication, and DWI. Snyder (1999) reports over 160,000 arrests of youth for alcohol-related charges in 1998, nearly eight percent of all arrests in that year.

Neither of the drug-related offenses nor vandalism were significant arrest predictors. This is an interesting coupling, since vandalism is normally a minor form of delinquency and drug sales a more serious one. Despite this, they share the commonality of secrecy. It is thus not a very surprising finding since such forms of delinquency are typically difficult for police to detect. School administrators, for example, may hesitate to report all cases of vandalism because they are trivial or fear it will reflect poorly on their managerial ability (Goldstein 1996). The modus-operandi for vandalism is likely to include the cover of darkness in the very late evening or early morning hours, whether for external damage to property (e.g. graffiti) or damage upon entry to an unguarded building. Similarly, drug use and drug deals are a form of deviance often taking place behind closed doors on private property. Even open-air drug markets operate with as much inconspicuousness as possible. Assaults and thefts are significant arrest predictors. As the more serious forms of delinquency, these results are as expected. Unlike drugs and vandalism, there is an immediate urgency presented by and for victims, who often press for investigation and police action, especially in assault cases. Moreover, a major shift in public school policy toward various forms of delinquency has resulted from the "zero tolerance" or Safe Schools Act implemented nationwide in the mid and late 1990's. Ever since, schools are more punitive in their handling of many forms of delinquency, but especially on those involving fighting and other forms of violence among students or when directed at teachers and staff. The main implication for many public middle and high schools is the increased use of law enforcement and formal juvenile justice processing for such infractions (Fries and DeMitchell 2007).

As expected, the effect of criminal history on arrests is positive and significant. It is the absolute strongest predictor in the model. Each increase in the number of arrests accumulated up to the year prior to each wave is associated with an increase of about one new arrest. Although criminal history does not appear in many juvenile arrest studies, it clearly is a critical part of the model, addressing delinquent propensity and "reputation" effects with police from the past encounter(s) or official labeling effects via instant computerized recall of arrest history in the field setting.

The choice to substitute criminal history for any number of social variables involving family and peer influences and difficulties in school is based on pre-tests determining that it accounts for much of the influence of these items. When prior arrest was entered with these items in earlier models (not shown), its effects were muted, as were the effects of the social items (i.e. statistical partialing effects). Opting for use of criminal history alone has resulted in a more parsimonious model.

DISCUSSION

A longstanding and ongoing federal initiative in the area of delinquency research is referred to as "Disproportionate Minority Contact (DMC)" with the juvenile justice system. The objective of this research program is to determine what causes DMC at various stages of involvement. A recent consideration of this effort is whether elevated delinquency among minority youth explains DMC, yet much of the existing research focuses on bias in the later stages of processing. Because the arrest decision is the ever-critical filter for the system, research that focuses on that front end of the process informs both theory and policy. If the primary deviation (i.e. delinquency) and propensity for delinquent involvement (prior arrests) are controlled, the results both inform theory and are useful to the policy debate.

The positive effect of racial minority status on arrest with key controls in place is clearly evidenced in this national sample of youth. Race effects were especially evident in petty crimes where police employ more discretion in making the arrest decision. Where one recent study using Rochester data finds minority effects on arrest by combining blacks and Hispanics (Hirschfield et al. 2006), the current study shows that running tests for these groups separately is a more informative approach. Labeling effects are more pronounced for black youth than for Hispanic youth. Demonstrating arrest bias against black youth generally upholds past findings, but with such sparse research on arrests of Hispanic youth, these results shed new light on ethnicity as a risk factor. This provides a benchmark for more specific investigations of the nature and form of the race-arrest relationship in subsequent chapters. The durability of these initial findings is now tested as SES enters the study.

CHAPTER 6:
SES and the Race-Arrest Relationship

INTRODUCTION

The analysis in Chapter 5 evidenced the main effect of race-ethnic minority status in increasing arrest risk. This is consistent with much of the literature on the role of black racial status in juvenile arrest and provides new findings on the labeling effect experienced by Hispanic youth. To continue moving this area of inquiry forward, the current chapter demonstrates whether and how these relationships can be explained or further specified by SES.

Informed by research that points to an appreciable overlap between racial minority status and poverty, SES is included in the model as a test item along with race. These items are also interacted to explore their combined effect on arrest risk. This chapter's analysis facilitates various tests of main and interaction statements in H_2 and H_3, again with Negative Binomial regressions.

MODELING

These models utilize two different measures of SES. Model 1 uses interviewer-rating of the neighborhood and home, dummied into High, Medium, and Low SES categories. Model 2 uses the natural log transformation of parent-reported household income (Sakamoto et al. 2000; Wilson 2000) at Wave 1. Having continuous values, it was mean-centered prior to being interacted with minority status in the final model (Jaccard et al. 1990). SES main effects are obtained by entering each SES measure in turn, in separate tests of H_2. This method also serves to evaluate the impact of SES on the race-arrest relationship. Interaction terms for Race $\times$ Rated-SES and Race $\times$ Income are then entered. A series of figures more clearly illustrates the form of these interactions, accompanied by proper significance tests.

Table 6.1 contains results for both SES models. The first column is the full race model carried over from Chapter 5. Rated-SES is entered in Column 2 to note its main effect on arrest (H_2) and to note its impact on the race-arrest relationship. High SES is the omitted category in Column 2. Income replaces Rated-SES in Column 3 in a re-assessment of H_2 and mediation effects. Race $\times$ Rated-SES interaction terms are added in Column 4 as a first test of H_3. Race $\times$ Income is then added in Column 5 in an alternate test of H_3.

RESULTS

Results in Columns 2 and 3 provide firm support for H_2. In Column 2, Low-SES significantly increased arrest risk, relative to High-SES, net of race and all other items. In switching SES indicators, Column 3 shows the effect of Income was in the expected direction (negative) and it was also statistically significant. Adding yet another demonstration of the interrelatedness of race and SES to the literature, both race-ethnic coefficients were weakened by the introduction of SES. The significance level of the Hispanic coefficient was reduced, further supporting the notion that black youth are labeled more intensely than Hispanic youth. Remaining items in the model are not much affected by the entry of SES.

Table 6.1: Arrests on Race, SES, and Interactions (n = 3,881)

	1 Full Race Model B (SE)	2 Rated SES B (SE)	3 Income SES B (SE)	4 Rated SES interact B (SE)	5 Income SES interact B (SE)
RACE					
White	–	–	–	–	–
Black	.465***	.333***	.417***	.585***	.427***
	(.120)	(.122)	(.121)	(.202)	(.124)
Hispanic	.284**	.213*	.240*	.523**	.255**
	(.128)	(.122)	(129)	(.202)	(.129)
DEMOGRAPHIC					
Male	.742***	.738***	.744***	.740***	.752***
	(.0105)	(.105)	(.105)	(.105)	(.105)
Age	-.038	-.039	-.041	-.038	-.040
	(.033)	(.033)	(.033)	(.033)	(.033)
Urban	.040	-.039	.025	-.026	.031
	(.107)	(.137)	(.107)	(.107)	(.107)
LEGAL					
Minor delinquency					
Alcohol use	.051***	.054***	.052***	.054***	.053***
	(.011)	(.014)	(.014)	(.014)	(.014)
Marijuana use	.028***	.027***	.027***	.027***	.027***
	(.009)	(.009)	(.009)	(.009)	(.009)
Hard drug use	.001	.001	.001	.001	.001
	(.001)	(.001)	(.001)	(.001)	(.001)
Vandalism	.054	.054	.044	.056	.039
	(.049)	(.048)	(.049)	. (.048)	(.050)
Serious delinquency					
Assault	.213***	.196***	.198***	.194***	.191***
	(.037)	(.037)	(.038)	(.037)	(.038)
Property crime	.223***	.218***	.230***	.210***	.232***
	(.036)	(.036)	(.036)	(.036)	(.036)

Table 6.1, Arrests on Race, SES, and Interactions (n = 3,881) (continued)

	1 Full Race Model B (SE)	2 Rated SES B (SE)	3 Income SES B (SE)	4 Rated SES interact B (SE)	5 Income SES interact B (SE)
Drug sales	.061 (.084)	.068 (.083)	.073 (.084)	.066 (.082)	.080 (.084)
Criminal history					
Prior arrests	1.12*** (.080)	1.07*** (.079)	1.10*** (.079)	1.06*** (.078)	1.10*** (.079)
Social class					
Low-SES rating	–	.974*** (.169)	–	.715** (.302)	–
Mid-SES rating	–	.376*** (.111)	–	.665*** (.150)	–
Log. Household Income	–	–	-.068*** (.025)	–	-.144*** (.041)
INTERACTIONS					
Black × Low-SES	–	–	–	.289 (.404)	–
Black × Mid-SES	–	–	–	-.582** (.267)	–
Hispanic × Low-SES	–	–	–	.130 (.451)	–
Hispanic × Mid-SES	–	–	–	-.652** (.279)	–
Black × Income	–	–	–	–	.119* (.068)
Hispanic × Income	–	–	–	–	.149** (.068)
Pseudo r-squared	.15	.16	.16	.16	.15

* p ≤ .10
** p ≤ .05
*** p ≤ .01

Untangling Race and SES Effects

Attempts at untangling the effects of race and SES, a common challenge in the crime literature, have uncovered many nuances in the complex relationship between these variables. To assist in that effort, this analysis examined mediation effects and in the next section, interaction effects between the two. The mediation findings suggested that the impact of SES on race effects depends in part on how SES is measured. Interviewer-rated SES attenuated race effects more than Income did. With rated SES entered in Column 2, the minority coefficients were reduced more than when income was used in Column 3.

Recall that rated SES was an index derived from interviewer remarks regarding the quality of youths' home and neighborhood. In a study of juvenile arrest, this type of measurement might be regarded as superior to a conventional measure that uses parental income, education, or occupation because it better approximates the patrol officer's perception-based assessment of SES. This is perhaps why it attenuated the race effect more than Income did. It appears that whatever was gleaned from the quality of the home and neighborhood explained more of the race-arrest relationship than did financial resources, a variable that is not directly observed by patrol officers.

Interaction Effects

In Column 4, interaction terms involving rated-SES failed to predict arrests for blacks or Hispanics, providing no preliminary support for H_3. Note, however that specifying this interaction strengthened minority main effects to their greatest magnitude across all models in the study to this point, a likely indication that the model is mis-specified without the interaction terms (Friederich 1982; Jaccard et al. 1990).

   While no hypothesis was stated for the mid-range SES category, it significantly interacts with minority status to reduce arrest risk, relative to the omitted category of High-SES minority subjects. Table 5.4 in Chapter 5 alluded to this relationship with the significant, positive race-arrest relationship evidenced among High-SES subjects only. Finally, interaction terms were significant using Income as SES in the final column of Table 3.[26] The following section more carefully probes the nature and form of these interactions for a clearer depiction of the interaction and proper tests of significance.

Probing the Race × Income Interaction

Obtaining the simple slopes by solving the regression equation with dummy variable values, taking the anti-log of coefficients to return them to their original units (annual arrest counts), and plotting results probes the significant interactions for a clearer demonstration of effects (Aiken and West 1991; Kaufman 2002). It is a way to determine whether conditional effects are truly present, while better illustrating the relational form of the values implied by the interaction. As a continuous variable, any values within the full range of income are eligible to model the simple slopes for race groups (Aiken and West 1991; Jaccard et al. 1990). The values selected were the log-transformed income value

---

[26] The significance reading for interaction terms in regression output is considered a global test of significance. In this case, it offers limited information, testing whether the interaction slopes are statistically different from zero, when all other variables have a value of zero (Aiken and West 1991; Jaccard and Turrissi 2003).

at one standard deviation above (1.75), and below (-1.75) the centered mean of zero.

Figure 6.1: Arrests on Race, Moderated by Income

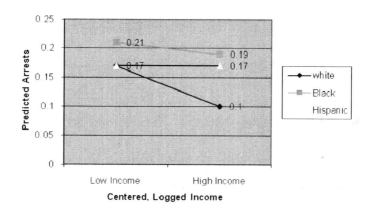

With Income as the moderator in this model, black and Hispanic main effects were estimates of the mean difference between each group and "whites" at the mean level of Income.[27] The interaction effects represent how this mean difference changed, given a one-unit increase in income (Jaccard and Turrisi 2003). In Figure 6.1, whites were the only group for which Income significantly

---

[27] In Figure 6.1, "white" actually represents white, female, non-urban respondents, slightly reducing the usefulness of its interpretation. This is due to the regression principle that the b_0 in the equation would normally be $\hat{Y}$ for the comparison group (here, whites) when all other independent variables equal zero (Jaccard and Turrisi, 2003). With other dummy items in the equation however (male and urban), the b_0 value represented $\hat{Y}$ for the *combination* of omitted dummy variable groups when all other independent variables equal zero.

reduced the effect of race on arrests (t = -3.48, p < .01). The
rate of decrease in the number of arrests created by Income
was not significant for blacks (t = -0.61) nor for Hispanics
(t = -0.01). The order of the variables are now switched to
examine how race moderated the income effect in Figures
6.2 and 6.3.

   Figure 6.2 shows that black racial status increased
arrest frequency by only 19 percent for Low-Income youth,
but increased it by 47 percent for High-Income youth, a
significant contrast (t = 3.09, p < .01), and opposite the
prediction made in H_3. Although race clearly moderated the
Income effect, this vantage point again illustrated that the
reverse was not true, i.e. Income did not substantially
moderate the race effect on arrest levels (right-hand side of
Figure 6.2).

Figure 6.2: Arrests on Income, Moderated by Race

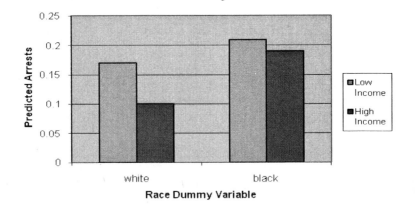

Conducting this test now for Hispanics, Figure 6.3 showed
some similarity to results for black youth, and one main

difference. While the effect of Hispanic ethnicity also raised the arrest risk for High-income youth (by 23 percent), the effect was not statistically different from the flat effect of the Hispanic × Low-SES interaction (t = 0.92). Finally, the right-hand side of Figure 6.3 reiterated that Income did not moderate the effect of ethnicity on arrest levels for Hispanic youth. Regression lines for both income groups converged at a predicted arrest value of .17 for Hispanics.

Figure 6.3: Arrests on Income, Moderated by Ethnicity

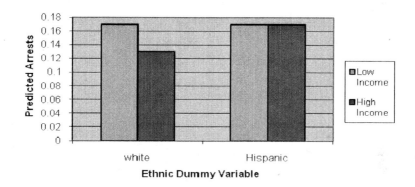

SUMMARY

This chapter tested two hypotheses regarding the role of race and SES on juvenile arrest frequency. There was clear support for H_2, the main effect of SES on arrests.

Coefficients were significant and in the expected direction for both SES measures (perceptual or income-based). SES did not fully explain the race-arrest relationship, but it did weaken it by about 25 percent with the perceptual measure and by about half that amount with

Income. These items were interacted to further explore the nature of their relationship to arrest.

Adding yet another entry to the ongoing effort to untangle race and class effects in crime and justice outcomes, preliminary results for hypothesized interactions (H_3) are contingent on which SES measure is used. Interacting race and perceptual SES did not yield significant regression results for blacks or Hispanics, but modeling the interaction with Income did. However, probing the simple slopes for Income illustrated that ultimately, it did not significantly condition the effect of race on arrests for minorities (Figure 6.1), failing to confirm preliminary significance results in Table 6.3.

Two key findings emerged in switching these moderator variables to note how race conditioned the effect of Income i.e. the other facet of the interaction. First, race mattered in arrest decisions for high-income youth. The arrest risk associated with being a high-SES Black youth was significantly larger than the risk associated with being white (High or Low-SES). Similarly, the arrest risk associated with being a High-SES Hispanic youth was larger than the risk experienced by their white counterparts. This is consistent with notions that minority youth are "out of place" in higher SES contexts. Several explanations may apply.

Minority subjects who engage in delinquency in high-SES areas may be under the extra watchful eye of neighbors and police, thus increasing their chance of arrest. If their dress, demeanor, and other symbolic cues are consistent with a delinquent youth subculture, they will draw attention to themselves in high-SES (and presumably socially organized) areas where there is less tolerance for such forms of deviance (Elliott et al. 1996; Sampson and Bartusch 1998). Another part of this story may be that some High-SES minority youth "hang out" in lower class neighborhoods to engage in delinquency. Not being from the neighborhood may result in out-of-place effects of a different sort, where they do not fit in and/or where police do not recognize them, establishing contact for that reason, driving up their chance for arrest. High-SES minority youth may also not be as adept as their Low-SES counterparts at avoiding detection by police for their misdeeds.

A second key finding was that minority status impacted the income-arrest relationship differently for blacks and Hispanics at low-income levels. The main difference is that Hispanic ethnic status failed to moderate the Low-SES-arrest relationship. Counter to expectations for this group, yet somewhat consistent with research on the paradoxical effect of poor Latino immigrant communities on crime outcomes, poverty had no effect on arrest risk for Hispanic youth.

CHAPTER 7

Gang Membership and Arrest: Specifying Race and SES Effects

INTRODUCTION

While gang membership has not received nearly as much attention in the labeling and arrest literature as race or class, its inclusion in this type of research is clearly warranted. Given the linkage of gang membership to elevated delinquency, the history of police-gang rivalry, and the widespread social disapproval of this deviant status, gang members ought to be among the most often arrested group of youth known to social science. Yet, there is limited empirical proof of this. Furthermore, it is unclear whether mere membership in a gang increases the risk of arrest or whether it must be accompanied by high levels of delinquency to have an effect. There are surprisingly few tests of the arrest risk associated solely with group membership. Of the few studies addressing this issue, there is more support for the idea that after controlling for legal and other relevant variables, gang membership is not a significant arrest predictor.

Given the ambiguities in the definition and measurement of gang membership, researchers ought not to take for granted the gang-arrest relationship. Use of a self reported gang measurement in a nationally representative sample of youth has the potential to include less-delinquent fringe members of the gang, as well as gang "wannabes", and can dilute the expected effect of gang membership on delinquency or arrest. As discussed in Chapter 3, only three studies have executed a critical test of the notion that gang membership is a risk factor for arrest, net of delinquency. This is the first study to examine the issue with national-level data.

This chapter's analysis begins with descriptive information on the full sample, delineated by gang membership status. The three hypotheses regarding the effect of gang membership on arrest risk are then tested with Poisson regression. I evaluate the main gang effect, net of race, SES, and controls (H_4) followed by Gang $\times$ Race (H_5) and Gang $\times$ SES (H_6) interactions.

DESCRIPTIVES

Table 7.1 provides descriptive data for all items in the analysis by gang membership status. The 299 gang members represents the total (n) of youth reporting active gang membership status in one or more of the four waves of data included in the study. Means in Table 7.1 are four-year averages. Consistent with prior research, minorities, males, and poor youth are significantly overrepresented in the gang population. As expected, delinquency and arrest levels are significantly higher for gang youth. One interesting exception is with hard drugs, where the slight difference in usage between the two groups is not ignify-cant. Marijuana use, however is much more prevalent among gang youth. Although it is largely characterized as an urban phenomenon in the gang research, the lack of a significant difference in the proportion of urban versus non-urban gang youth lends support to growing evidence of

Table 7.1: Sample Characteristics by Gang Membership Status

	Full Sample (n) of persons = 3,881		Gang Member n = 299		Non-Gang n = 3,582	
	Mean	s.d.	Mean	s.d.	Mean	s.d.
Arrested	.05	.22	.27*	.44	.04	.20
Arrests	.079	.46	.58*	1.57	.06	.38
RACE-ETHNICITY						
White	.54	.50	^.34*	.47	.54	.50
Black	.24	.43	.30*	.42	.23	.46
Hispanic	.21	.41	.36*	.48	.21	.41
DEMOGRAPHIC						
Male	.52	.50	.77*	.42	.50	.50
Age	15.21	1.61	15.27	1.53	15.17	1.61
Urban	.39	.49	.43	.39	.39	.49
LEGAL						
Minor Delinquency						
Alcohol Use	.78	2.72	2.82*	5.5	.66	2.53
Marijuana Use	.92	4.22	5.51*	9.86	.72	3.66
Hard Drug Use	3.64	44.5	4.95	67.1	3.62	44.2
Vandalism	.26	.90	1.26*	1.94	.23	.85

Table 7.1: Sample Characteristics by Gang Membership Status (Continued)

	Full Sample (n) of persons = 3,881		Gang Member n = 299		Non-Gang n = 3,582	
	Mean	s.d.	Mean	s.d.	Mean	s.d.
Serious Delinquency						
Assault	.24	.95	1.94*	2.48	.19	.82
Property Crime Index	.28	1.11	1.76*	3.06	.24	.97
Drug Sales	.07	.44	.54*	1.17	.06	.38
Criminal History						
Prior Arrests	.12	.70	.73*	2.22	.09	.48
SES Interviewer Rating						
Low	.07	.25	.11*	.32	.07	.26
Mid	.42	.47	.58*	.49	.41	.49
High	.51	.48	^.30*	.46	.52	.50
Wealth						
Gross HH Income - (in thousands)	$46.6	37.2	^$30.0*	30.2	$48.1	41.7

* Signicantly different from non-gang mean at p < .05, ** p < .01 in a 2 sample t-test with equal variances.
^ t-value for group is negative

the spread of gangs to non-urban areas (Evans et al. 1999; Greene and Pranis 2007; Weisheit and Wells 2004).

GANG MODELS

The logic of this chapter's multivariate analysis is similar to that of the previous chapter. One main difference is the baseline model contains both race and SES, making the main effect test for gang membership the most stringent among the three test items in the study. As before, legal items are added in three separate blocks followed by equations containing the interaction terms.

Main Effects

Consistent with the expectation that gang youth engage in frequent and serious delinquency, results in Table 7.2 show that the gang effect on arrest is somewhat attenuated with the entry of delinquency and criminal history. Yet, the positive, significant effect of gang membership status holds up beyond the entry of these legal items, in support of H_4. With conflicting results reported for Seattle and Chicago in past research on this issue (albeit possibly due to a period-effect), the current study is in agreement with Curry's (2000) results from Chicago.

Several recent findings from the juvenile gang research show that gang membership is a mediator for delinquency (McNulty and Bellair 2003; Vigil 2002). Some mediation effects in Table 7.2 are apparent between gang membership and several delinquency variables thought to be related to the youth gang subculture.

Table 7.2: Arrests on Gang Status, Controls, and Interactions

	1 Gang Baseline B (SE)	2 Minor Delinq. B (SE)	3 Serious Delinq. B (SE)	4 Criminal History B (SE)	5 Gang × Race B (SE)	6 Gang × SES b (SE)
Gang Member	1.82** (.084)	1.07** (.093)	.738** (.100)	.398** (.104)	-.474* (.195)	1.13** (.189)
RACE-ETHNICITY						
White	—	—	—	—		
Black	.060 (.071)	.303** (.071)	.299** (.072)	.404** (.072)	.273** (.076)	.496** (.081)
Hispanic	-.028 (.074)	.121 (.074)	.124 (.074)	.209** (.074)	.082 (.081)	.274** (.085)
DEMOGRAPHIC						
Male	.903** (.066)	.785** (.067)	.767** (.067)	.670** (.068)	.644** (.069)	.734** (.079)
Age	.102** (.018)	.041* (.019)	.027 (.019)	-.023 (.020)	-.036 (.020)	-.024 (.022)
Urban	.220** (.061)	.126* (.062)	.090 (.062)	.031 (.062)	-.049 (.063)	.114 (.071)
SES						
Low	1.12** (.091)	1.12** (.091)	1.01** (.092)	.940** (.092)	.947** (.093)	1.18** (.109)
Medium	.513** (.068)	.466** (.068)	.477** (.068)	.315** (.070)	.325** (.070)	.409** (.085)

Table 7.2: Arrests on Gang Status, Controls, and Interactions (Continued)

	1 Gang Baseline B (SE)	2 Minor Delinq. B (SE)	3 Serious Delinq. B (SE)	4 Criminal History B (SE)	5 Gang × Race B (SE)	6 Gang × SES b (SE)
LEGAL *Minor Delinquency*						
Alcohol Use	—	.061** (.005)	.061** (.005)	.049** (.005)	.050** (.005)	.061** (.006)
Marijuana Use	—	.042** (.004)	.035** (.005)	.042** (.005)	.037** (.005)	.018** (.004)
Hard Drug Use	—	-.012 (.016)	-.018 (.017)	-.062** (.018)	-.043* (.018)	.002** (.000)
Vandalism	—	.192** (.017)	.053* (.023)	.098** (.022)	.104** (.022)	.168** (.024)
Serious Delinquency						
Assault	—	—	.131** (.016)	.144** (.022)	.141** (.017)	.136** (.019)
Property Crime	—	—	.097** (.014)	.067** (.014)	.069** (.014)	.024 (.016)
Drug Sales	—	—	-.014 (.031)	.051 (.032)	.063* (.031)	.124** (.036)
Criminal History						
Prior Arrests	—	—	—	.225** (.009)	.255** (.011)	.250** (.012)
INTERACTIONS						
Gang × Black	—	—	—	—	1.43** (.244)	—
Gang × Hispanic	—	—	—	—	1.06** (.227)	—
LowSES × Gang	—	—	—	—	—	- 1.89** (.410)
Mid-SES × Gang	—	—	—	—	—	-.439 (.228)
Pseudo r-squared	.09	.14	.16	.19	.20	.23

* p ≤ .05 ** p ≤ .01

Whereas vandalism was not a significant arrest predictor prior to the entry of gang membership into the study, it now is. Hard drug use and drug sales obtain similar effects in interactions equations (discussed below). With these exceptions, results for all other demographic and legal items are durable across the various models. Interestingly, when not included in the baseline model, but when entered separately, neither Rated-SES nor Income explain much of the gang effect on arrests (results not shown). Recalling from the previous chapter that SES attenuates the race-ethnic effect, it has a different relationship with gang membership. The absence of mediation effects between gang status and SES was quite unexpected, given the considerable overlap of these variables in past research.

Interaction Effects

In Column 5 of Table 7.2, the Gang × Race interaction is positive and significant for both minority groups, offering preliminary support for H_5.[28] With the interactions included, the main effect of gang membership reflects its influence on arrests when race equals zero (i.e. the omitted group, white), and thus it is negative, an indication that gang effects are conditioned by race. Gang membership as a risk factor for arrest (H_4) is still intact since in the presence of an interaction, the main effect of its constitutive terms is considered an "average" effect (Jaccard et al. 1990). Where gang membership is primarily a minority phenomenon in these data, the overall gang effect had thus far masked the particular effects for white gang youth.

---

[28] See note #26 regarding simple slope significance testing.

Rather than to make a definitive prediction about the effect of the Gang × SES interaction, recall that in Chapter 4, competing hypotheses were articulated. The first, H_{6a} was the "intuitive" hypothesis that gang membership will have a stronger positive effect on arrest for Low versus High-SES youth. The alternative or "paradoxical" hypothesis (H_{6b}) made the opposite prediction that gang membership will have a stronger positive effect on arrests for High SES youth.

Results in Column 6 provide preliminary support for H_{6b}, the alternative (paradoxical effects) hypothesis. The Gang × Low SES interaction in Column 6 is negative and significant. The next section more carefully probes the nature and form of the Gang × Race and Gang × SES interactions for a clearer depiction of the various relationships among these variables.

Probing Interactions

Gang × Race

As with the interaction models in Chapter 6, this section probes the test item interactions for the current chapter. In Table 7.2, the Gang × Race interaction was positive and significant for both minority groups, offering preliminary support for H_5. Results in Figure 7.1 provide firm support for the black youth component of H_5, as racial minority status drastically moderates the relationship of gang membership status to arrests. Among gang members, the slope for black youth is 82 percent larger than that of white youth, but among non-gang youth, it is only 23.5 percent larger. The difference between these simple slopes is significant ($t = 3.94$, $p < .01$). Also note that arrests for white gang youth are predicted to be *lower* than for non-gang white youth, a finding that was also reflected in the negative main effects gang coefficient in Column 5 of Table 7.2.

Figure 7.1: Arrests by Gang Status, Moderated by Race

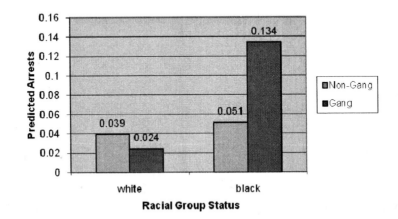

Switching the order of variables in Figure 7.2 illustrates that gang membership also significantly moderates the race effect. Again H_5 is supported, as gang membership status increases the expected number of arrests for black youth by 62 percent and as noted in Table 7.2, *decreases* predicted arrest frequency for white youth by 38 percent, a substantive contrast and a significant difference (t = 6.29, p < .01).

The Gang × Hispanic interaction in Figure 7.3 shows that Hispanic ethnicity drastically moderates the relationship of gang membership status to the number of arrests. In support of H_5, among gang youth, the Hispanic slope is 68 percent larger than the white slope and for non gang youth, it is only 7 percent larger, a significant result (t = 3.24, p < .01). As with black youth, the contrast between predicted arrests for Hispanic gang youth and non-gang Hispanic youth is very pronounced.

Figure 7.2: Arrests by Race, Moderated by Gang Status

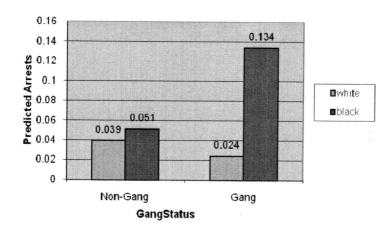

Figure 7.3: Arrests by Gang Status, Moderated by Ethnicity

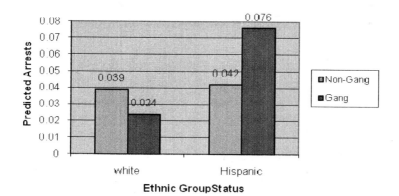

Finally, Figure 7.4 shows that gang membership increases the expected number of arrests by 45 percent for Hispanic youth, contrasted with the standard decrease in predicted arrests by 38 percent for white youth, a significant difference (t = 4.13, p < .01). Like the Gang × Black interaction, Figures 7.3 and 7.4 show that Gang × Hispanic obtains interaction effects in both directions (i.e. each item significantly moderates the effects of the other).

Figure 7.4: Arrests by Ethnicity, Moderated by Gang Status

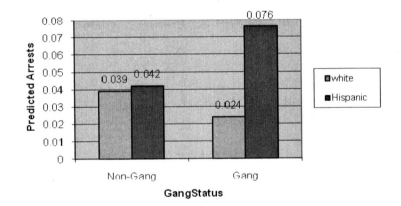

Gang × SES
Turning now to tests of H_6, a number of interesting findings emerge. Interactions coefficients in Table 7.2 were consistent with the alternative or "paradoxical" hypothesis (H_{6b}) that gang membership will have a stronger positive effect on arrests for High SES youth than for other groups. Results in Figure 7.5 show that indeed, gang membership conditions the relationship of SES to arrest frequency in

this manner. In the *non-gang* population, the effect of SES is predicted to be about three times as large for Low versus High SES subjects. Among gang members, however, the relationship reverses and High SES now increases arrest frequency by about double that of Low SES. Gang membership thus drastically moderates the SES-arrest relationship, increasing predicted arrests among High SES subjects by 67 percent, a significant difference relative to non-gang High SES subjects (t = 5.98, p < .01), demonstrating a very particular type of "out of place" effect. Gang Membership also conditions the Low SES–arrest relationship, reducing its impact on arrest frequency by about 50 percent (t = -2.06, p < .05), indicating a direct "protective" effect.

Figure 7.5: Arrests by SES, Moderated by Gang Status

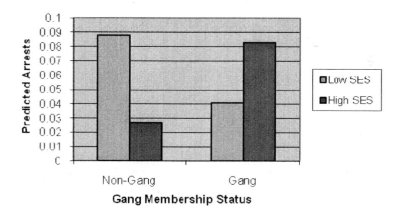

Switching variables in Figure 7.6 illustrates that SES also significantly moderates the gang effect, evidence of symbiotic interaction effects. The paradoxical hypothesis is again supported, as the effect of High SES on arrest frequency for gang youth is about 50 percent greater than the effect of Low SES, a significant difference (t = 7.02, p < .01).

Figure 7.6: Arrests by Gang Membership Status, Moderated by SES

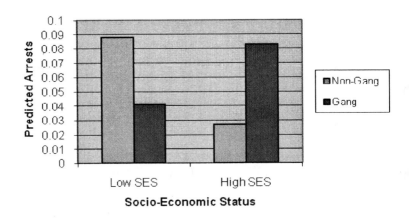

SUMMARY AND CONCLUSION

Prior research has all but neglected the question of whether gang members experience arrest risks beyond what is warranted by their delinquency level (i.e. labeling effects). After conflicting findings across the few study sites that have executed this test, the answer remained in dispute. Attempting to bring some resolution to this issue with survey data for the nation, the first multivariate analysis in this chapter found support for an undue arrest risk experienced by gang members.

Based on the recent trend toward criminalization of active gang member status, with many places in the U.S. enacting civil gang injunctions as a suppression tactic, these results are not all too surprising. Indeed, the policy of targeting gang youth for arrest may be more defensible than the targeting of minority youth, but the great overlap in these populations serves to complicate the matter substantially. While they are often the signifiers of gang membership, it is not the subcultural elements such as race, group cohesiveness, gang apparel, etc. that are criminalized *per se*, but elevated criminal behavior that makes these youth the target of suppression. With delinquency and criminal history controlled in these models, however, the most distinguishing characteristic of gang membership is removed (theoretically at least), arguably leaving only its social components.

Given that street gangs predominate in minority communities, the absence of any studies to date that examined the interaction of gang membership and race on juvenile arrests is surprising. This chapter helped to fill that gap and to bring new insights to the effort to discover sources of DMC with the justice system. Results were as predicted in H_5, and were extremely robust, as Gang Membership and minority status both conditioned the effects of the other on arrest.

The Gang Membership × SES interaction provides a most interesting set of paradoxical results, given the direction of main effects and the cogent theoretical premises accompanying the more "intuitive" hypothesis. Figure 7.5 shows that self-reported gang youth whose SES was rated High by NLSY97 interviewers are penalized for this dual status in terms of arrest risk, relative to Low SES gang youth and High SES non-gang youth. Inasmuch as poverty and gang membership overlap with racial minority status, results show that the contours of DMC with regard to arrest risk are complex and even somewhat counter-intuitive.

CHAPTER 8:

Conclusion—Labeling and the Confluence of Extralegal Characteristics on Juvenile Arrest

INTRODUCTION

Racial profiling and differential treatment of minorities by police has been an issue of great concern to justice scholars and practitioners for the past several decades. Although the issue has received much recent research attention, little is known about its specific manifestations, or whether it even exists at all. The labeling perspective predicts that the disproportionate targeting of certain minority groups by police is systematic enough to be statistically significant after controlling for legal variables. Conducting this type of investigation with a focus on youth contributes to the ongoing federal DMC research initiative and addresses police-minority group relations generally.

While race has been the primary element of profiling considerations, this area of inquiry has expanded (or rather reverted by conflict theory) to consider that profiling also operates on the basis of social class. Informed by much research that points to the interrelatedness of race and social class, SES played a major role in the study. Its main, mediation, and conditional effects with race and arrest were modeled for black and Hispanic youth. Its complex

119

relationship with gang membership and arrest was also demonstrated. Like race and class, the inclusion of gang membership in the study provided valuable insights on labeling dynamics involved in the arrests of youth. Notions of the profiling of gang youth for arrest proved to be salient in the findings. While this area has not received nearly as much attention in the labeling or arrest literature as race and class, it is clearly related to both of these variables in juvenile arrest dynamics.

The various analyses in this book collectively served to evaluate the utility of labeling theory in explaining the arrest of juveniles. The first task required identifying a set of relevant legal and extralegal factors potentially affecting a subject's risk of arrest. With sufficient controls in place, the unique contributions to arrest risk posed by the study's test items are interpreted as "labeling effects."

DISCUSSION OF FINDINGS

The Race-Ethnic Labeling Hypothesis

Results from Chapter 5 convincingly establish that the link between race-ethnic minority status and arrest is present in a representative sample of American teenagers. Results of all critical tests allowed for blanketed evaluations of "minority" effects in several models, but overall, labeling effects are slightly stronger for blacks than for Hispanics, underscoring the importance of running tests for these groups separately. Looking back across all regression models, the black slope was significant more often than the Hispanic slope and it was more durable in the presence of other test items and controls.

The differences between black and Hispanic youth were also evident when SES entered the picture in Chapter 6. SES attenuated race effects about equally for both minority groups, but the significance level for Hispanic coefficients was reduced in several equations. Then, when race was interacted with SES, the "out-of-place" results from simple slope analysis were significant for blacks only. Given the sparse research on Latinos and arrest, this study provided some noteworthy insights. Placing these findings in a wider context, several of the remaining challenges and limitations in developing this area of research are offered below.

Hispanic Youth

This study represents what is surely one of the first national-level examinations of the arrest risk posed by the juvenile's Hispanic ethnicity status. The few studies addressing this question do so for youth in individual cities and most are rather dated. Thus, no real benchmark exists to compare against the current findings, but results are generally consistent with other research on Hispanic involvement with crime and the justice system. A common theme in system treatment of Hispanics is that they experience mid-range levels of punishment, relative to blacks and whites (California Administrative Office of the Courts 2001; Hebert 1997; Mustard 2001; Royo-Maxwell and Davis 1999; Tapia and Harris 2006). Although the margin of differential labeling between race groups is not great in the current study, Hispanic youth are clearly not labeled to the same degree as black youth.

Reasons for the lack of research on Latinos and arrest are both logistical and conceptual. The lack of official arrest data is the primary impediment to researching Latinos and crime in general. It is worth noting however, that this data limitation may be due, in part to reliability issues with Latino offenders.

The reliability with which a suspect's ethnicity is ascertained in criminal episodes, especially those not resulting in quick apprehension is not known. Even the advanced stages of criminal justice processing have problems with identifying and properly coding Hispanic subjects (Barela-Bloom and Unnithan 2009; Hagan and Palloni 1999). The issue for offender reports is that while race is often discernable by sight, (i.e. skin color or other distinguishing physical features), in theory, ethnicity is not. Ethnicity mainly refers to cultural elements such as language use and the country(ies) from which a person's ancestry may be traced (Hawkins, Laub, Lauritson, and Cothern 2000; Hutchinson and Smith 1996; Tonry 1997; Yinger 1985). Presumably, phenotype varies too widely among Hispanics for their ethnic group status to be reliably discerned by sight.

In the National Crime Victimization Survey (NCVS) for example, the survey respondent (victim) reports the perceived race of lone offenders with whom they have visual or physical contact. Yet, the offender's *ethnic* group status is apparently not considered to be reliably discerned by the victim in these scenarios, hence this data item is not collected. In neither of the nation's two official crime reporting databases, the Uniform Crime Report or the National Incident-Based Reporting System, is the reporting of Hispanic arrest data mandatory for local agencies.

A potential source of error in the current study then was police inability to identify a subject's racial or ethnic group status by relying on perceptual cues such as skin tone, language proficiency, etc. While this issue pertains to all racial minority populations, it is most salient with Latinos and is perhaps the main reason official crime reporting systems do not record offense and arrest information on them. As an *ethnic* group, Hispanics may theoretically be distributed across the four major race categories,[29] therefore official offender data are not available for the Hispanic designation (Gabiddon and Greene 2009; Morenoff 2005; Sissons 1979; Walker et al. 2003).

Some may consider it absurd to suggest that Latinos are indistinguishable from whites, blacks, Asians, or other groups, both on a visual basis, and especially in situations where police become aware of a subject's Spanish surname, a Spanish language accent, etc. Theorizing on the treatment of Latinos by police might also consider how the level of race-ethnic residential segregation might impact the targeting or differential treatment of Latinos by police (i.e. "anti-gang" directives that saturate the barrio with patrol).

On the other hand, if phenotype is thought to vary so widely among Hispanics, it may be difficult for police to visually discern their "Hispanicity", thereby mitigating the probability of being targeted for arrest on this basis. Indeed, as over 90 percent of Hispanics are coded as "white" in Census data, this is probably also true of how Hispanics are coded in official crime data.

Another limitation common to many datasets is the failure to measure the diversity within the Latino category. This is true of the data used for the current study, resulting in my treatment of the Hispanic category essentially as a major race group to be compared with blacks and whites. Like most national-level youth surveys, the NLSY97 does

---

[30]. Although in Census data, over 90 percent were white (U.S. Census Bureau, 2010).

not specify Latino sub-groups. Yet, the racial and cultural diversity within the Hispanic category is well noted, even in crime studies (Martinez 2002; Morenoff 2005; Nielsen et al. 2005; Morenoff and Astor 2006; Rumbaut et al. 2006; Urbina 2007). The most useful distinction is nationality (e.g. Cuban, Mexican, Puerto Rican), which encompasses many of the cultural differences within the larger Hispanic group. Potentially important variation in the arrest risk associated with Latino subgroups is therefore masked in the current study.

Socio-Economic Status (SES)

Results for the labeling effect of SES on arrests of youth (H_2) were among the more definitive of the study's findings, with significant slopes in the predicted direction for both SES-based models in Chapter 6. For both interviewer-rating of the neighborhood and home and parent-reported annual household income, results echoed many recent findings on juvenile arrest in studies that also used survey data.

The Confluence of Race and SES in Juvenile Arrest Research

Piecing apart the effects of race and SES is a common challenge in the crime literature. This analysis examined both mediation and interaction effects to inform that effort. The findings suggested that the way SES is measured can impact race effects on arrest. One nuance was that interviewer-rated SES attenuated effects for both minority groups more than Income did. The interviewer's perceived SES measurement might be regarded as preferable to a conventional measure because it more closely proxies the patrol officer's perception-based assessment of SES.

However, as an interaction term, Rated-SES did not perform as well as Income. Interaction terms involving rated-SES failed to predict arrests for blacks or Hispanics, providing no preliminary support for H_3. Interaction terms were only significant with Income as SES in the final model in Chapter 6.

Two key findings emerged from in-depth probing of this interaction. First, race mattered in arrest decisions for high-income youth. The arrest risk associated with being a High-SES black youth was significantly larger than the risk associated with being white (High or Low-SES). Similarly, the arrest risk associated with being a High-SES Hispanic youth was larger than the risk experienced by their white counterparts (albeit not significantly). Despite the lack of statistical significance for Hispanics, the substantive findings are consistent with notions that minority youth are "out of place" in higher SES contexts.

Minority subjects who engage in delinquency and who live in High-SES areas may come under extra scrutiny by members of their community, thus increasing their chance of arrest. Their youthful misgivings may draw more attention than those of their counterparts in Low-income neighborhoods where there is more tolerance for deviant behavior.

Another critical finding was that minority status impacted the income-arrest relationship differently for blacks and Hispanics at low-income levels. The main difference is that ethnicity failed to moderate the low-SES-arrest relationship for Hispanics. Echoing the research on the paradoxical effect of poor Latino immigrant communities on criminological outcomes (Martinez, 2002; Morenoff, 2005; Nielsen et al., 2005; Sampson et al., 2005; Sampson and Bean, 2006; Velez, 2006; 2009), poverty did not increase the risk of arrest for Hispanic youth. Alternative modeling in future research may find this effect to be fully paradoxical (i.e., where poverty exerts a "protective" feature against arrest) relative to the risk of arrest experienced by other race-class combinations.

Gang Membership
One of the more difficult hypotheses to commit to (resulting in a highly qualified statement) was whether youths' gang membership status alone would increase their risk of arrest. Labeling theory responds with a forceful "yes" to this question, perhaps even more-so than for race or SES-based labeling. This is because the menace of gang membership represents some of the least socially desirable by-products of poor, minority contexts, and because the very definition of gang member connotes criminality. However, measurement issues and findings from previous studies casted some doubt on the gang labeling effect.

In the current framework, the antithesis to labeling theory is the legal perspective on the cause of arrest. It holds that it is not one's status as a racial minority, a poor person, or a gang member that increases arrest chances, but one's behavior. If the defining feature of "gang member" is frequency or seriousness of delinquent behavior, then it is logical to target them for arrest. In short, the prevailing belief about police response to the existence of gangs is that membership in a criminal enterprise makes them a public enemy and it is "open season" on these youth (Katz and Webb 2006). An interesting caveat is that not all gang-involved youth engage in high levels of delinquency. In fact some report engaging in none at all. Table 1 in Appendix B shows that of 250 youth who maintained gang member status throughout all four years of the study, 13 percent (n = 33) reported no delinquency over the same period.

Of course, on average, gang youth engage in more delinquency than non-gang youth. Table 2 of Appendix B shows that the delinquency level of gang youth was about five times higher than that of non-gang youth. However, a comparison of the range and variation of self-reported delinquency is also important in determining whether gang youth deserve to be targeted for arrest with such vigor. Note the higher standard deviation in delinquency scores among gang youth, indicating a wide variation in offending levels. The non-gang youth exhibit more regularity in their levels of offending, but with a much higher ceiling, due to outliers.

With multiple regression, equal levels of delinquency is simulated for gang and non-gang youth for hypothesis testing. Results show that belonging to a gang increases the chances of getting arrested, independent of the youth's offending characteristics and criminal history, a robust finding. Moreover, with such legal variables controlled in these models, the most distinguishing characteristic of gang membership is removed (theoretically at least), arguably leaving only the social components of membership. Ultimately, this labeling effect was not a surprising finding, given the trend toward criminalization of gang member status in many U.S. places.

The Gang Member of Color Hypothesis

Results from this study suggest that a good amount of labeling of youth by police in the U.S. exists in the form of the targeting of gang members of color. This finding is consistent with prior research on the coexisting effects of minority and gang status on arrest risk, but the lack of any prior examination of their interaction on juvenile arrests was surprising. Rather dynamic interactions for Race × Gang emerged, especially when gang membership status is the moderator variable. Results show that gang membership increases the predicted number of arrests for minority youth while *decreasing* the number of arrests for whites. That the youth gang population is overwhelmingly a racial-ethnic minority one makes these results all the more poignant. Not only are these relationships very robust, but they affect many minority youth in America's inner cities (Greene and Pranis 2007). Although in the current study, gang membership is antecedent, these arrest-based findings also complement, in part, the notion of "multiple marginality" experienced by gang youths in the social structure (Freng and Esbensen 2007; Vigil 2002). Finally, because gangs are more likely to come from disadvantaged contexts (Curry and Spergel 1988, Esbensen and Huizinga 1993; Sampson 1986; Thornberry et al. 2003), exploring the nexus between social class and gang membership help to more fully address the notion of multiple arrest risk.

Gang Membership, SES, and Juvenile Arrests

Part of the rationale for specifying the Gang × SES interaction in this study is informed by historical notions of the intersection of poverty and delinquent subculture (e.g. Shaw and McKay). Neighborhoods where these elements are present are, in turn, disproportionately comprised of racial minorities (Farrington et al. 2003; Kaufman, 2005; McNulty and Bellair 2003; Peeples and Loeber, 1994; Wikstrom and Loeber 2000). Here is where the effects of "multiple marginality" were truly expected to emerge.

However, in the arrest context, these effects did not fully manifest in the most intuitive manner.

Interaction effects for SES × Gang obtained paradoxical findings consistent with research on the "out of place" phenomenon for High-SES gang youth, and protective effects for Low-SES gang youth. The finer contours of labeling processes in arrest suggest that when High SES youth affiliate themselves with the gang lifestyle (either in or out of their own neighborhood), they are subject to increased chances for arrest. This "out of place" effect could reflect resentment on the part of their neighbors and/or police that these youth are trying to be something they are not.

Although similar effects have been evident in studies of racial profiling of black motorists and black youth in higher SES contexts, "out of place" effects are seldom noted for gang youth in particular. Moreover, previous work on gangs was qualitative in nature, making the current study's findings the first glimpse of this type of effect in quantitative research.

Turning to the protective feature of gang membership for youth from poor neighborhoods, the effect of this dual status is predicted to be half as strong as that of High SES Gang status, and Non-Gang Low SES status. Several gang-related processes that likely contribute to this finding are the effect of restricted movement of gang youth within neighborhood boundaries to avoid attacks by rivals, thereby reducing contact with police; possible "lookout effects" (Patillo-McCoy 1999); and the "stealthy criminals" effect (Dunford and Elliott 1984).

A careful interpretation of these interactions results must first take into account that arrest levels for gang youth and poor youth are already elevated, as indicated by their main effects. That the main effects for race, gang membership, and SES remain strong and significant in the presence of the significant interaction is also important and informative. Despite the paradoxical findings, these suggest that elements of the multiple marginality expectation are still somewhat intact. For example, although they assume the role of control variables in this part of the research, (Chapter 7) race-ethnic based labeling effects are clearly evident in the gang models. In the end, that main effects for gang, SES, and race effects robustly emerge after controlling for key legal and demographic items indicates that some part of the increased arrest risk experienced by socially marginalized groups is unwarranted. In short, if after controls are in place, the focal variables still increase the risk of arrest, then these characteristics mean something more to the police, likely equating to increased scrutiny and harsher treatment. The current trend of criminalizing gang membership, absent instant delinquency charges or outstanding arrest warrants causes the interaction of gangs, SES, and race in the earliest stages of DMC to go undiscovered and unaddressed. If these practices continue to go unchecked, the disproportionate arrest of poor, minority youth is likely to persist.

STUDY LIMITATIONS

Arrest incidents are defined by a host of legal and extra-legal variables that are often complexly related. To date, no single dataset or study measures them all, however. Often, a methodological choice must be made between obser-vations of police-juvenile contacts in the field, official data, and/or survey data. Whereas the merits of survey data in evaluating labeling theory and showing it is a useful framework for understanding juvenile arrest were demonstrated here, data limitations disallow a full picture of arrest dynamics. Field observations capture important idiosyncratic elements that are either not measurable with the self report method or are often not documented or sufficiently detailed in official reports. Witness statements, complainant demands for arrest, the presence of evidence (Black and Reiss 1970), suspect demeanor (Brown et al. 2009; Lundman 1996; Novak et al. 2002; Reisig et al. 2004; Piliavin and Briar 1964; Werthman and Piliavin 1967; Worden et al. 1996), encounter location (Smith 1986), officer's race (Brown et al. 2009) and the presence of onlookers (Reisig et al. 2004) are all critical elements that help determine the course of action taken by police. Variation in police department policies on how to handle incidents involving juveniles adds another degree of complexity in predicting arrest (Bell and Lang 1985; Black and Reiss 1970; Cicourel 1976; Monahan 1970; Terry 1967).

In this vein, a measure of simple police contact was not available in the NLSY97. The regression coefficients and simple slope tests are not telling of the sheer volume of contacts between police and youth of various races, social classes, etc., but simply the level of arrest risk associated with these various race-class statuses. Yet, recent works on this topic suggested that perhaps due to their disproportionately low-SES, minority youth generally experience more police contact, which increases their chances for arrest (Jones-Brown 2000; Russell-Brown 2009). Before assuming differential treatment or profiling of minority youth, this is one of the potential underlying causes of disproportionate minority arrests. Thus, regardless of the method employed, it is truly difficult to disentangle race and class effects.

While Race × Gang results were very robust for both minority groups in Chapter 7, future research on this topic might expand the range of delinquent acts on either end of the offense severity spectrum. Minority and gang youth often live in inner city contexts where the "street code" milieu is prevalent and where issues related to defensive posturing and self protection are germane (Anderson 1999; Matsueda et al. 2006). The lack of a weapons carrying item as an arrestable offense may thus be suppressing Minority × Gang labeling effects in the current analysis. On the other end of the offense severity spectrum, because the gang is often depicted as an extension of, or surrogate for, the family unit (Miller 1958; Miller 2001; Moore 1992; Padilla 1992; Vigil 2002), runaway is a potentially salient form of delinquency for gang youth. Its absence in an arrest study may also be suppressing Race × Gang effects.

Another option for modeling the Race × Gang effect is to follow the cohort into higher age groups. One reason for choosing the sample I did was tied to the belief that some delinquency measures used as legal controls here would not be appropriate for older teens and young adults in their twenties. The concern was that the qualitative nature of offenses for older youth, and older gang youth especially, would no longer be well-captured by traditional delinquency measures (namely vandalism and minor theft). Older youths' contact with police is more likely to involve or coincide with traffic stops, for example. Forms of offending in the young adult gang arena are also sure to involve more drug crimes, and in turn, more violence (Valdez 2006).

To address such concerns, future research might use more recent waves of data, and may focus on arrests for particular types of crimes such as drug selling and assault.

If drug gangs or gang-involved drug dealers thrive in minority and poor communities, one might expect for more vigorous monitoring of minority gang members by police working in those places. While the current design obtained cogent results to suggest that use of the Gang × Race interaction is a good measure for modeling arrest risk such refinements and extensions of the research may be beneficial.

Despite the limitations of the current study, the merits of longitudinal survey data to investigate arrests of youth are now recognized by contemporary researchers of the juvenile justice system, even though such surveys were not specifically designed to do so (Huizinga et al. 2007). Utilizing detailed self reports about substance use and involvement in delinquent behavior directly addresses the claim that higher minority contact with police is due to their higher rates of delinquency. As seen in this and other recent longitudinal studies on the topic (Hirschfield et al. 2006; Huizinga et al. 2007), the race effect on arrest is sustained past delinquency and the powerful effect of prior arrests.

IMPLICATIONS FOR POLICY AND THEORY

The policy implications of this work link to the ongoing federal research initiative known as "disproportionate minority contact (DMC)" with the juvenile justice system. The goal of this research program for the past twenty years has been to determine what causes DMC at various stages of involvement (Office of Juvenile Justice and Delinquency Prevention, 2010 b). The most recent priority of this effort is examining youths' earliest point of contact with the juvenile justice system, but so far arrest research has been scarce. Much DMC research focuses on later stages in the processing of youth through the justice system and uses the secondary labeling framework to theorize about the life trajectory and identity forming consequences of involvement with the system (Gove 1975). Because the arrest decision is the ever-critical filter for the system, however, research that focuses on the primary labeling process as a selection mechanism is especially important to conduct.

A point of debate in the current DMC dialogue is whether minority youth simply engage in more delinquency, warranting higher levels of contact (Huizinga et al., 2007; OJJDP 2010 b; Piquero, 2008). Evidence of this was mixed in Table 5.4 in Chapter 5, but to be sure, a model that accounts for minority overrepresentation in any particular crime type (assault in the current study) is needed. If the primary deviation (i.e. delinquency), and propensity for the primary deviation (prior arrests) have been controlled and extralegal effects remain, the results must be considered robust for their ability to withstand such rigorous partialling.

The method used to explore the effects of extralegal variables on arrest is also a test of labeling theory. It is an appropriate theoretical framework for interpretation because its antithesis is essentially that delinquent intensity should explain arrest levels. Hence, the modeling solution to rule out that possibility is quite simple. The straightforward task of controlling for delinquency makes this, in the end, a study of police bias. The results inform this police-labeling paradigm, where the increased chances of certain youth to be arrested for characteristics not inherently legal in nature is tantamount to differential treatment by police, if not profiling.

The tension between labeling and legal perspectives, while somewhat antithetical, is not a zero-sum game. In order to avoid confounding the effects of extralegal labeling on arrest risk, one must control for legal items. Indeed, the most basic notion of arrest risk is one that relies on an estimate of one's arrest eligibility, or the number of times one is willing to risk the odds of getting caught for illegal behavior. Clearly, the more harm done to the victim, the more society's control agents will seek justice in the form of incapacitation and punishment of the offender, especially for predatory crimes. It is when the legal basis for making arrests is weak and extralegal factors become as or more salient that police action strays from the justice ideal.

The conflict-based strands of labeling theory used here posit that this, in turn, tempers police-minority group relations. Some might even argue that it helps to perpetuate the relatively low social position of race and ethnic minorities. The current research adds to this paradigm, suggesting the selection process involved in arrest unduly targets the poor communities minority youth disproportionately inhabit, and the vilified subcultures that are disproportionately comprised of minorities. When these social forces interact, multiple risk effects for arrest result.

General Delinquency Measures, 12-Month Incidence

Item and (Original Scale)	Recode	Index Score	Mean / Skewness*	
			Original Scale	Recode
Destroy Property	0	0		
(0 - 99)	1	1		
	2	2		
	3	3	} 0.46 / 18.6	0.20 / 5.0
	4	4		
	5	5		
	6-10	6		
	11- 99	7		
Steal < $50	0	0		
(0 - 99)	1-2	1		
	3-9	2	} 0.68 / 14.2	0.15 / 3.8
	11 – 99	3		
Steal > $50	0	0		
(0 – 99)	1	1		
	2	2		
	3-4	3	} 0.26 / 22.7	0.08 / 7.6
	5-9	4		
	10 – 99	5		

Item and (Original Scale)	Recode	Index Score	Mean / Skewness*	
			Original Scale	Recode
Handling Stolen Property (0 – 99)	0	0		
	1	1		
	2	2		
	3	3	} 0.22 / 22.8	0.07 / 7.5
	4-9	4		
	10 – 99	5		
Attack/Assault (0 – 99)	0	0		
	1	1		
	2	2		
	3	3	} 0.44 / 18.9	0.24 / 5.0
	4	4		
	5	5		
	6-10	6		
	11 - 99	7		
Sell Drugs (0 – 99)	0	0		
	1-3	1		
	4-9	2	} 1.40 / 8.6	0.10 / 6.2
	10-20	3		
	21-98	4		
	99	5		

* Means and Skewness statistics averaged over 4 waves

Delinquency By Gang Member Status

Table B.1: Four-year Delinquency Status by Four-year Gang Member Status

Delinquency	Current Gang Member	
	No	Yes
No	8,936 (65.1%)	33 (13.2%)
Yes	4,781 (34.9%)	217 (86.8%)

(n) of stacked person-period observations (4 years) minus missing data = 13,967

Table B.2: Four-year Delinquency Score by Four-year Gang Member Status

	(N)	Mean	Standard Dev.	Range
Non Gang	13,717	9.89	85.09	0 - 3001
Gang Member	250	48.43*	122.62	0 - 997

Two-sample t-test with equal variances t = 7.03 * p < .001

Bibliography

Aiken, Leona, and Stephen West. 1991. *Multiple Regression: Testing and Interpreting Interactions.* Newbury Park, CA: Sage Publications.

Akers, Ronald L. 1998. *Social Learning and Social Structure: A General Theory of Crime and Deviance.* Boston: Northeastern University Press.

Allan, Edward. 2004. *Civil gang abatement: the effectiveness and implications of policing by injunction.* New York: LFB Scholarly.

Allison, Paul D. 2002. *Missing Data.* Thousand Oaks, CA: Sage.

Alpert, G., Dunham, R., and Smith, M. 2007. "Investigating racial profiling by the Miami-Dade Police Department: A multi-method approach." *Criminology and Public Policy* 6: 25-55.

Anderson, Elijah. 2000. *Code of the Street: Decency, Violence and the Moral Life of the Inner-City.* New York: W. W. Norton and Company.

Ball, R. A. and Curry, G. D. 1995. "The Logic of Definition in Criminology: Purposes and Methods for Defining Gangs." *Criminology* 33: 225-245.

Barrows, Julie and C. Ron Huff. 2009. "Constructing and Deconstructing Gang Databases" *Criminology and Public Policy*, 8(4): 675-701.

Battin, Sara, Karl G. Hill, Robert Abbott, Richard Catalano, J David Hawkins. 1998. "The contribution of Gang Membership to Delinquency Beyond Delinquent Friends." *Criminology* 36: 93-116.

Barela-Bloom, C and Unnithan, P. 2009. Hispanics and juvenile court disposition: A County-level study. *Criminal Justice Studies, 22*(3), 331-344.

Bayley, David and Harold Mendelsohn. 1969. *Minorities and the Police: Confrontation in America.* New York: The Free Press.

Becker, Howard 1963. *Outsiders: Studies in the Sociology of Deviance.* New York: The Free Press.

Bell, Duran and Kevin Lang. 1985. "The intake dispositions of juvenile offenders." *Journal of Research in Crime and Delinquency* 22(4): 309-328.

Bellair, Paul E. and Thomas L McNulty. 2005. "Beyond the Bell Curve: Community Disadvantage and the Explanation of Black-White Differences in Adolescent Violence." *Criminology* 43(4): 1135-69.

Bernburg, J. G., Marvin D Krohn, Craig J Rivera. 2006. "Official labeling, criminal embeddedness, and subsequent delinquency: a longit test of labeling theory." *The Journal of Research in Crime and Delinquency* 43(1):67.

Bjerregaard, B., and Alan J. Lizotte 1995. "Gun Ownership and Gang Membership" *The Journal of Criminal Law and Criminology* (86): 37-58.

Black, Donald, and Albert Reiss. 1970. "Police Control of Juveniles." *American Sociological Review* 35: 63-77.

Bostaph, L. G. 2007. Race and repeats: The impact of officer performance on racially biased policing. *Journal of Criminal Justice* 35: 401-417.

Brown, Robert A., Novak, Kenneth J., and James Frank. 2009. "Identifying variation in police officer behavior between juveniles and adults." *Journal of Criminal Justice* 37: 200-208.

Brownfield, D., Ann Marie Sorenson and Kevin Thomson. 2001. "Gang Membership, Race, and Social Class: A Test of the Group Hazard and Master Status Hypothesis." *Deviant Behavior* 22: 73-89.

Brownfield, D. and K.M. Thompson 1991. "Attachment to peers and delinquent behaviour." *Canadian Journal of Criminology* 33(1): 45-60.

Brownfield, D and Thompson, KM 2002. "Distinguishing the effects of peer delinquency and gang membership on self-reported delinquency." *Journal of Gang Research* 9: 1-10.

Brownfield, D., K. M., Thompson, Sorenson, A. 1997. "Correlates of gang membership: A test of strain, social control, and social learning theories." *Journal of Gang Research* 4:11-22.

Brunson, R. K., and Weitzer, R. (2009). Police relations with Black and White youths in different urban neighborhoods. *Urban Affairs Review*, 44: 858-885.

Bureau of Justice Statistics Bulletin. 2002a. "Prisoners in 2002" Report NCJ200248 http://www.ojp.usdoj.gov/bjs/pub/pdf/p02.pdf

Bureau of Justice Statistics Bulletin 2002b. "Probation and Parole in the U.S. 2002" Report NCJ201135. http://www.ojp.usdoj.gov/bjs/pub/pdf/ppus02.pdf

Bursik, Robert J., Jr. and Harold G. Grasmick. 1993. *Neighborhoods and Crime: The Dimensions of Effective Community Control.* New York: Lexington Books.

Butts, Jeffrey and Howard M. Snyder 2006. "Too soon to tell: deciphering recent trends in youth violence." *Chapin Center for Children,* Univ. of Chicago. Issue Brief #110: 1-8.

California Administrative Office of the Courts. 2001. "Report to the Legislature: The Disposition of Criminal Cases According to the Race and Ethnicity of the Defendant."

Cameron, Colin and Pravin Trivedi. 1986. "Econometric Models Based on Count Data." *Journal of Applied Econometrics.* 1(1): 29-53.

Cameron, Colin and Pravin Trivedi. 1998. *Regression Analysis of Count Data.* New York: Cambridge University Press.

Center for Human Resource Research. 2007. *A guide to rounds 1-9 of data.* U.S. Dept. of Labor. www.nlsinfo.org

Chambliss, William. 1973. "Race, Sex, and Gangs: The Saints and Roughnecks." *Transaction* 11: 24-31.

Chesney-Lind, Meda. 1978. "Young women in the arms of the law." In: Bowker, L. (ed.), *Women, Crime, and the Criminal Justice System.* Lexington MA: Heath.

Chesney-Lind, M. 1999. "Trends in Women's Crime." Ch 12 In: Scarpitti and Nielsen (eds), *Crime and Criminals.*

Chesney-Lind, M., Rockhill, A., Marker, N., Reyes, H. 1994. "Gangs and Delinquency." *Crime, Law, and Social Change* 21: 201-228.

Cicourel, Aaron. 1976. *The Social Organization of Juvenile Justice.* New York: Wiley and Sons.

Cloward, Richard A. and Lloyd E. Ohlin. 1960. *Delinquency and Opportunity: A Theory of Delinquent Gangs.* New York: The Free Press.

Cohen, Albert K. 1955. *Delinquent Boys: The Culture of the Gang.* Glencoe: The Free Press.

Curry, David G. 2000. "Self-reported gang involvement and officially recorded delinquency" *Criminology* 38(4): 1253-1273.

Curry, David G. and Irving A. Spergel 1988. "Gang Homicide, Delinquency, and Community" *Criminology* 26(3): 381-405.

Curry, David G. and Irving A. Spergel 1992. "Gang involvement and delinquency among Hispanic and African-American adolescent males." *The Journal of Research in Crime and Delinquency* 29 (3): 273-291.

Dannefer, Dale and Russell Schutt. 1982. "Race and Juvenile Justice Processing in Court and Police Agencies." *American Journal of Sociology* 87(5): 1113-1132.

Decker, Scott and Barrik Van Winkle 1996. *Life in the Gang.* New York, NY: Cambridge University Press.

DeFleur, Lois 1975. "Biasing influences in drug arrest records: implications for deviance research." *American Sociological Review* 40(1): 88-103.

Dukes, Richard, Martinez, Ruben O., and Judith A. Stein 1997: "Precursors and consequences of membership in youth gangs" *Youth and Society* 29: 139-165.

Dunford F., and Elliott, D. 1984. "Identifying Career Offenders using Self Reported Data." *Journal of Research in Crime and Delinquency.* 21: 57 – 86.

Elliott, Delbert S. and Suzanne S. Ageton. 1980. "Reconciling Race and Class Differences in Self-Reported and Official Estimates of Delinquency." *American Sociological Review* 45(1): 95-110.

Elliott, Delbert S., Huizinga, David, and Susanne Ageton. 1985. *Explaining Delinquency and Drug Use.* Beverly Hills, CA: Sage. Ch's 1-4.

Elliott, Delbert S., Huizinga, David and Barbara Morse. 1987 "Self-Reported Violent Offending: A descriptive analysis of juvenile violent offenders and their offending careers." *Journal of Interpersonal Violence* 1: 472-514.

Elliott D., W.J. Wilson, Huizinga R.J., Sampson, Elliott A., and Rankin B. 1996. Effects of Neighborhood Disadvantage on Adolescent. Development." *Journal of Research in Crime and Delinquency* 33: 389-426.

Elliott, Delbert S. and Harwin Voss. 1974. *Delinquency and Dropout.* Lexington, MA: DC Heath.

Empey, Lamar. 1982. *American Delinquency: Its Meaning and Construction.* Homewood, IL: Dorsey.

Engel, Robin. 2005. "Citizens' Percenptions of Distributive and Procedural Injustice During Traffic Stops with Police." *Journal of Research in Crime and Delinquency,42(2) 445-481.*

Erickson, Maynard. 1971. "The group context of delinquent behavior." *Social Problems* 19: 114-129.

Esbensen, F.A., Thomas Winfree Jr., Ni He, and Terrance Taylor. 2001. "Youth gangs and definitional issues:

when is a gang a gang and why does it matter?" *Crime and Delinquency* 47: 105-130.

Esbensen, Finn-Aage and David Huizinga. 1993. "Gangs, Drugs and Delinquency in a survey of Urban Youth." *Criminology* 31: 565-587.

Evans, William, Fitzgerald, Carla, Weigel, Dan, and Sarah Chvilicek. 1999. "Are Rural Gang Members Similar to Their Urban Peers?" *Youth and Society* 30(3): 267-282

Farrington D.P., Loeber R., Stouthamer-Loeber M., Kammen W.B.V., Schmidt L. 1996. "Self-reported delinquency and a combined delinquency seriousness scale based on boys, mothers, and teachers: concurrent and predictive validity for African-Americans and Caucasians." *Criminology* 34(4): 493-518.

Farrington, David P., Rolf Loeber, and Magda Stouthamer-Loeber. 2003. "How can the Relationship between Race and Violence be Explained?" pp. 213-37 in Darnell F. Hawkins (ed.) *Violent Crime: Assessing Race and Ethnic Differences*. New York: Cambridge University Press.

Farrington, David P., Jolliffe, Darrick, Hawkins, J. David, Catalano, Richard F., Hill, Karl G. and Rick Kosterman. 2010. "Why Are Boys More Likely to be Referred to Juvenile Court? Gender Differences in Official and Self-Reported Delinquency" *Victims and Offenders*, 5(1): 25-44.

Federal Bureau of Investigation, 2004. "Arrest of Juveniles for Drug Abuse Violations 1994-2003" in *Crime in the U.S. Uniform Crime Reports.* Washington, D.C.: U.S. Government Printing Office.

Ferdinand, Ted and Elmer Luchterhand. 1970. "Inner city youth, the police, the juvenile court, and justice." *Social Problems* 17(4): 510-527.

Fischer, Claude S. 1995. "The Subcultural Theory of Urbanism: A Twentieth Year Assessment." *American Journal of Sociology* 101(3): 543-77.

Fitzmaurice, Garrett, M., Laird, Nan M., and James H. Ware. 2003. *Applied Longitudinal Analysis*. Hoboken, NJ: Wiley & Sons.

Freng, Adrianne and Finn Aage Esbensen. 2007. "Race and Gang Affiliation: An Examination of Multiple Marginality." *Justice Quarterly* 24(4): 600-628.

Friedrich, Robert. 1982. "In Defense of Multiplicative Terms in Multiple Regression Equations." *American Journal of Political Science* 26: 797-833.

Fries, Kim and Todd DeMitchell. 2007. "Zero Tolerance and the Paradox of Fairness: A View from the Classroom." *Journal of Law and Education* 36(2): 211-229.

Gabiddon, Shaun. and Greene, Helen T. (2009). *Race and crime* (2nd ed.). Thousand Oaks, CA: Sage.

Giallombardo, Rose. 1980 "Female Delinquency" in Shichor, D. and Kelly, D.H. (eds.) *Critical Issues in Juvenile Delinquency*. Lexington, MA: Heath.

Goffman, Irving. 1963. *Stigma: Notes on the Management of Spoiled Identity*. Englewood Cliffs, N. J.: Prentice-Hall.

Gold, M. 1966. "Undetected delinquent behavior." *Journal of Research in Crime and Delinquency* 3: 27-46.

Goldstein, Arnold. 1996. *The Psychology of Vandalism.* New York: Plenum Press.

Goode, Erich. 1975. "On behalf of labeling theory." *Social Problems* 22(5): 570-583.

Gordon, Rachel, Lahey, Ben, Kawai, Eriko, Loeber, Rolf, Stouthhamer-Loeber, Magda, and David Farrington. 2004. "Antisocial Behavior and Youth Gang Membership: Selection and Socialization." *Criminology* 42(1): 55-88.

Gottfredson, Michael and Travis Hirschi 1990. *A General Theory of Crime*. Palo Alto, CA: Stanford University Press.

Gould, Leroy 1969. "Who Defines Delinquency? A Comparison of Self Reported and Officially-Reported Indices of Delinquency for Three Racial Groups." *Social Problems* 16(3): 325-336.

Gove, Walter. 1975. "The labeling of deviance: Evaluating a perspective." New York: Sage.

Greene, J. and K. Pranis. 2007. "Gang Wars: The Failure of Enforcement Tactics and the Need for Effective Public Safety Strategies." *Justice Policy Institute Report*.

Grogger, Jeffrey. 2005. "What we know about gang injunctions." *Criminology and Public Policy*, 4, 637-642.

Hagan J., and McCarthy, W. 1992. "Streetlife and delinquency." *British Journal of Sociology* 43: 533-561.

Hagedorn, John. 1988. *People and Folks: Gangs, Crime, and the Underclass in a Rustbelt City*. Chicago: Lakeview Press.

Hebert, C. (1997). "Sentencing outcomes of Black, Hispanic, and white males convicted under Federal sentencing guidelines." *Criminal Justice Review 22*: 133-156.

Heimer, Karen and Ross L. Matsueda. 1994. "Role-taking, Role Commitment, and Delinquency: A Theory of Differential Social Control." *American Sociological Review* 59: 365-90

Henry, David B. Patrick H. Tolan, and Debra Gorman-Smith. 2001 "Longitudinal family and peer group effects on violent and non-violent delinquency" *Journal of Clinical Child Psychology* 30: 172-186.

Hill, Karl, Lui, Christina, and J. David Hawkins. 2001. "Precursors of Gang Membership." OJJDP *Juvenile Justice Bulletin*, NCJ 190106.

Hindelang, M.J., T. Hirschi, and J.G. Weis. 1979. Correlates of Delinquency: The illusion of discrepancies between self report and official msrs of delinquency." *American Sociological Review* 44 (6):995-1014.

Hindelang, M. Hirschi, T., and Weiss, J. 1981. *Measuring Delinquency*. Beverly Hills, CA: Sage.

Hirschel, J. D., Dean, C. W., and Dumond, D. 2001. Juvenile curfews and race: A cautionary Note. *Criminal Justice Policy Review, 12*(3): 197-214.

Hirschfield, P., T. Maschi, H.R.White, L.G. Traub, and R. Loeber. 2006. "Mental Health and Juvenile Arrests: Criminality. Criminalization, or Compassion?" *Criminology* 44(3): 593-627.

Hirschi, Travis. 1969. *Causes of Delinquency*. Berkeley, CA: UC Press.

Horowitz, Ruth. 1983. *Honor and the American Dream: Culture and Identity in a Chicano Community*. New Brunswick, N.J.: Rutgers University Press.

Howell, James, J. Moore, and A. Egley, Jr. 2001. "The Changing Boundaries of Youth Gangs." In: Ronald Huff, ed., *Gangs in America 3rd Edition*. Thousand Oaks, CA.: Sage.

Huff, C. Ronald. 2002. "Wrongful Conviction and Public Policy." *Criminology* 40 (1):1-18.

Huff, C. Ronald. 1996. "The Criminal Behavior of Gang Members and Nongang At-Risk Youth." pp. 75-102 in C. Ronald Huff (ed.), *Gangs in America 2nd Edition*. Thousand Oaks, CA.: Sage.

Huizinga and Elliott 1987. "Juvenile Offenders: Prevalence, offender incidence, and arrest rates by race." *Crime and Delinquency* 33: 206-223.

Huizinga, D., T. Thornberry, K. Knight, and P. Lovegrove. 2007. "Disproportionate Minority Contact in the Juvenile Justice System: A Study of Differential Minority Arrest/Referral to Court in Three Cities." Unpublished Report to the Office of Juvenile Justice and Delinquency Prevention.

Jaccard, James, Turrisi, Robert. 2003. *Interaction Effects in Multiple Regression*, 2nd ed. Newbury Park, CA: Sage.

Jaccard, James, Turrisi, Robert, and Choi K. Wan. 1990. *Interaction Effects in Multiple Regression*. Newbury Park, CA: Sage.

Jackson, Pamela I. 1989. *Minority Group Threat, Crime, and Policing: Social Context and Social Control*. New York: Praeger.

Jackson, Robert K. and Wesley D. McBride. 1996. *Understanding Street Gangs*. Incline Village, NV: Copperhouse.

Johnston, Jack and John DiNardo. 1997. *Econometric Methods*. 4th ed. New York: McGraw-Hill.

Katz, Charles, Vincent Webb and David Schaeffer. 2001 "The validity of police gang intelligence lists: examining differences in delinquency between documented gang members and non-documented delinquent youth." *Police Quarterly* 3:4.

Katz, Charles and Vincent Webb. 2006. *Policing Gangs in America*. New York: Cambridge.

Kaufman, Joanne. 2005. "Explaining the race/ethnicity–violence relationship: Neighborhood context and social psychological processes." *Justice Quarterly* 22(2): 224-251.

Kaufman, Robert. 2002. Didactic Seminar, *Interpreting Interactions* taught at the 2002 American Sociological Association Annual Meeting.

Kempf-Leonard, Kimberly, Pope, Carl, and William Feyerherm. 1995. *Minorities in juvenile justice*. Thousand Oaks, CA: Sage Publications.

Kent, S. L. and D. Jacobs. 2005. "Minority Threat and Police Strength from 1980 to 2000: A Fixed Effects Analysis of Non-Linear and Interactive Effects in Large U.S. Cities." *Criminology* 43(3): 731-756.

Klein, Malcom. 1995. *The American Street Gang*. New York: Oxford University Press.

Klein, Malcolm. 2004. *Gang Cop: The words and ways of Paco Domingo*. Walnut Creek, CA: Alta Mira Press.

Klein, Malcolm. 2009. "Bootlegging: A Career Caught Between Fantasy and Reality." *Criminology and Public Policy*, 8(1): 1-12.

Klinger, David. 1997. "Negotiating order in Patrol Work: an ecological theory of police response to deviance." *Criminology* 35(2): 277-306.

Kornhauser, Ruth. 1978. *Social Sources of Delinquency: Underlying Assumptions of Basic Models of Delinquency Theories*. Chicago : University of Chicago Press. Chapters 1-3.

Land, Kenneth, Patricia McCall and Lawrence Cohen. 1990. "Structural Covariates of Homicide Rates: Are There Any Invariances Across Time and Space?" *American Journal of Sociology* 95: 922-963.

Lattimore, Pamela K., Visher, Christy, and Richard Linster. 1995. "Predicting Rearrest for Violence Among Serious, Youthful Offenders." *Journal of Research in Crime and Delinquency* 32(1): 54-83.

Lattimore, Pamela K., John M. McDonald, Alex Piquero, Richard L. Linster, and Christy Visher. 2004. "Studying the Characteristics of Arrest Frequency Among Paroled, Youthful Offenders." *Journal of Research in Crime and Delinquency* 41: 37-57.

Laub, John. 1981 "Ecological Considerations in Victim Reporting to the Police." *Journal of Criminal Justice* 9(6): 419-430.

Lemert, Edwin M. 1951. *Social Pathology*. New York: McGraw-Hill.

Levin, Shana and Colette van Laar. 2006. *Stigma and Group Inequality*. Mahwah, NJ: Erlbaum.

Long, J. Scott. 1997. *Regression Models for Categorical Models and Limited Dependent Variables*. Thousand Oaks, CA: Sage.

Long, Scott and Jeremy Freese. 2003. *Regression Models for Categorical Variables Using Stata*. College Station, Texas: Stata Press.

Ludwig, J., Duncan, G.J., Hirschfield, P. 2001. "Urban Poverty and Juvenile Crime: Evidence from a Randomized Housing Mobility Experiment." *Quarterly Journal of Economics* 116(2): 655-679.

Lundman, Richard. 1996. "Demeanor and arrest: additional evidence from previously unpublished data." *Journal of Research in Crime and Delinquency* 33: 306-323.

Lundman, R., Sykes, R., and J. P. Clark. 1978. "Police Control of Juveniles, A Replication." *Journal of Research in Crime and Delinquency* 15: 74-91.

Lynam, D. R., Caspi, A., Moffitt, T., Wikstrom, P. O., Loeber, R., and Scott Novak. 2000. "The Interaction Between Impulsivity and Neighborhood Context on Offending: The Effects of Impulsivity are Stronger in Poor Neighborhoods." *Journal of Abnormal Psychology*, 109(4): 563-574.

Males, M. and Macallair, D. 1999. An analysis of curfew enforcement and juvenile crime in California. *Western Criminology Review 1*(2), [Online] Available, http://wcr.sonoma.edu/v1n2/males.html.

Mann, Coramae R. and Marjorie S. Zatz, eds. 1995. *Images of Color, Images of Crime*. Los Angeles: Roxbury.

Martinez, Ramiro. Jr. 2002. *Latino Homicide: Immigration, Violence, and Community*. New York: Routledge.

Martinez, Ramiro Jr. and Abel Valenzuela, eds. 2006. *Immigration and Crime: Race, Ethnicity, and Violence*. New York: New York University Press.

Matthews, Shelley, K. and Robert Agnew. 2008. "Extending Deterrence Theory: Do Delinquent Peers Condition the Relationship Between Perceptions of Getting Caught and Offending?" *Journal of Research in Crime and Delinquency* 45(2): 91-118.

Matsueda, R. and K. Heimer. 1987. "Race, Family Structure, and Delinquency." *American Sociological Review* 52: 826-840.

Matsueda, Ross, Kevin Drakulich and Charis Kubrin. 2006. "Race and Neighborhood Codes of Violence." In: Ruth Peterson, Lauren Krivo and John Hagan (eds.), *The Many Colors of Crime: Inequalities of Race, Ethnicity and Crime in America*. New York: NYU Press.

Matza, David. 1964. *Delinquency and Drift*. New York: The Free Press.

Maxfield, M.G., Weiler, B.L., and Widom, C.S., 2000. "Comparing self reports and official records of arrest" *Journal of Quantitative Criminology* 16: 87-110.

Maxson, C. Hennigan, K. M., and Sloane, D. C. 2005. "It's getting crazy out there: Can a civil gang injunction change a community?" *Criminology and Public Policy*, 4, 577-606.

McCall, Patricia, Land, Kenneth, and Karen Parker 2010. "An Empirical Assessment of What We Know About the Structural Covariates of Homicide Rates: A Return to a Classic 20 Years Later." *Homicide Studies* 14(3): 219-243.

McCorkle, R. and Miethe, T. 1998. "The political and organizational response to gangs: an examination of a 'moral panic' in Nevada." *Justice Quarterly* 15: 41-64.

McEachern, A.W. and R. Bauzer 1967. "Factors related to disposition in juvenile police contacts." In Klein and Myerhoff (Eds.) *Juvenile Gangs in Context*. Englewood Cliffs, NJ: Prentice-Hall.

McNulty, Thomas and Paul Bellair. 2003. "Explaining racial and ethnic differences in serious adolescent violent behavior." *Criminology* 41(3): 709-748.

Meehan, Albert and Michael Ponder. 2002. "Race and Place: The ecology of racial profiling African American motorists." *Justice Quarterly* 19(3): 399-430.

Menard, Scott, and Delbert Elliott. 1990. "Longitudinal and Cross-Sectional Data Collection and Analysis in the Study of Crime and Delinquency." *Justice Quarterly* 7:11-55.

Miller, Jody. 2001. *One of the Guys: Girls, Gangs and Gender*. "Gangs and Gang Life in Columbus." New York: Oxford University Press.

Miller, Walter. 1958. "Lower class culture as a generating milieu of gang delinquency." *Journal of Social Issues* 14: 5-19.

Monahan, Thomas. 1970. "Police Dispositions of Juvenile Offenders." *Phylon* 31(2): 129-141.

Moore, Joan. 1991. *Going Down to the Barrio: Homeboys and Homegirls in Change*. Philadelphia: Temple University Press

Morash, Merry 1983. "Gangs, Groups, and Delinquency." *British Journal of Criminology*, 33(4): 309-335.

Morenoff, J.D.2005 "Racial and ethnic disparities in crime and delinquency in the US." In: Tienda M, Rutter M, eds. *Ethnicity and Causal Mechanisms*. New York, NY: Cambridge University Press.

Morenoff, J. and Astor, A. (2006). "Immigrant Assimilation and Crime: Generational Differences in Youth Violence In Chicago." In: Martinez, Ramiro. Jr. and Abel Valenzuela, eds, *Immigration and Crime.* New York: NYU Press, 36-63.

Morris, N.A., and Slocum, L.A. 2010. "The validity of self-reported prevalence, frequency, and timing of arrest." *Journal of Research in Crime and Delinquency*, 47: 1-31.

Mustard, David B. 2001. "Racial, Ethnic and Gender Disparities in Sentencing: Evidence from the US Federal Courts." *The Journal of Law and Economics,* 44(1): 285-314.

Myers, Stephanie. 1999. "Police encounters with juvenile suspects: explaining the use of authority and provision of support." Washington D.C.: National Institute of Justice.

Nagin, Daniel and D.P. Farrington. 1992. "The Stability of Criminal Potential from Childhood to Adulthood." *Criminology* 30(2): 236-260.

Nagin, D. and R. Paternoster. 1991. "On the Relationship of Past to Future Participation in Delinquency." *Criminology* 29(2): 163-189.

NLSY Topical Guide: Age of Respondent. http://www.nlsinfo. org/nlsy97/nlsdocs/nlsy97/ topicalguide/age.html

NLSY Topical Guide: Geographic Indicators. http://www.nlsinfo.org/nlsy97/nlsdocs/nlsy97/ topicalguide/geogind.html

National Poverty Center. 2007. "Poverty in the U.S." http://www.npc.umich.edu/poverty/

National Youth Gang Center. 2007. http://www.iir.com/ nygc/

Nielsen, Amie, Matthew T. Lee and Ramiro Martinez, Jr. 2005. "Integrating Race, Place and Motive in Social Disorganization Theory: Lessons from a Comparison of Black and Latino Homicide Types in Two Immigrant Destination Cities." *Criminology* 43(3): 837-872.

Novak Kenneth and Mitch Chamlin. 2011. "Racial Threat, suspicion, and police behavior: Race, place, and Traffic Enforcement." Forthcoming in *Crime and Delinquency*.

Novak, S., J. Frank., B. Smith, R. Engel. 2002. "Revisiting the decision to arrest: Comparing beat and community officers." *Crime and Delinquency* 48: 70-98.

Nye, F. I. and J. F. Short, Jr. 1956. "Scaling Delinquent Behavior." *American Sociological Review* 22: 326-331.

Office of Juvenile Justice and Delinquency Prevention (OJJDP) 2010a. Statistical Briefing Book. http://ojjdp.ncjrs.org/ucr

Office of Juvenile Justice and Delinquency Prevention (OJJDP) 2010b. Disproportionate Minority Contact. http://www.ojjdp.ncjrs.gov/ dmc/

Osgood, D. Wayne, and Jeff Chambers. 2003. "Community Correlatos of Rural Youth Violence." *Juvenile Justice Bulletin*, May: 1-12.

Ousey,Graham and Matthew R. Lee. 2008. "Racial Disparity in Formal Social Control." *Journal of Research in Crime and Delinquency* 45(3): 322-355.

Padilla, Felix. 1992. *Gangs as an American Enterprise.* New Brunswick, N.J.: Rutgers University Press.

Paternoster, R. and Leeann Iovanni. 1989. "The labeling perspective and delinquency: an elaboration of the theory and an assessment of the evidence." *Justice Quarterly* 6(3): 359-394.

Patillo-McCoy, Mary. 1999. *Black Picket Fences*. Chicago: University of Chicago Press.

Peeples, Faith and Rolf Loeber 1994. "Do Individual Factors And Neighborhood Context Explain Ethnic Differences In Juvenile Delinquency?" *Journal of Quantitative Criminology* 10(2): 141-157.

Piliavin, Irving and Scott Briar 1964. "Police Encounters with Juveniles" *American Journal of Sociology* 70: 206-214

Piquero, Alex R. 2008. "Disproportionate Minority Contact." *The Future of Children Journal*, 18, 59-79.

Piquero, Alex. and Robert Brame. 2008. "Assessing the Race-Ethnic Crime Relationship in a Sample of Serious Adolescent Delinquents." *Crime and Delinquency* 54(3): 390-422.

Piquero, Alex, Brezina, Tim, and Michael Turner. 2005. "Testing Moffitt's Account of Delinquent Abstention" *Journal of Research in Crime and Delinquency*, 42(1): 27-54.

Pope, Carl, and Howard Snyder. 2003. "Race as a Factor in Juvenile Arrests." *Juvenile Justice Bulletin* NCJ 189180.

Puzzanchera, Charles. 2009. "Juvenile Arrests 2008." *Juvenile Justice Bulletin* NCJ 228479.

Quinney, Richard. 1970. *The Social Reality of Crime*. Boston: Little, Brown

Quinney, Richard. 1974. *Critique of Legal Order: Crime Control in a Capitalist Society*. Boston: Little, Brown.

Rabe-Hesketh, Sophia and Brian Everitt. 2007. *A Handbook of Statistical Analyses Using STATA*. Boca Raton, FL: Chapman and Hall.

Raskin White, Helene, Peter C. Tice, Rolf Loeber and Magda Stouthamer-Loeber. 2002. "Illegal Acts Committed by Adolescents Under the Influence of Alcohol and Drugs." *Journal of Research in Crime and Delinquency* 39(2):131-152.

Reisig, Michael D., John D. McCluskey, Stephen D. Mastrofski, and William Terrill. 2004. "Citizen Disrespect Toward the Police." *Justice Quarterly* 21(2): 241-268.

Rennison, Callie Marie. 2002. "Hispanic Victims of Violent Crime, 1993-2000." Bureau of Justice Statistics *Special Report* NCJ 191208.

Roche, K.M. Ensminger, M.E., and A.J. Cherlin. 2007. "Variations in parenting and adolescent outcomes among African american and latino families living in low income urban neighborhoods." *Journal of Family Issues* 28(7): 882-909.

Rosenthal, Lawrence. 2000. "Gang Loitering and Race." *Journal of Criminal Law and Criminology* 91:99-160.

Royo-Maxwell, S., and Davis, J. 1999. The salience of race and gender in pretrial release decisions: A comparison across multiple jurisdictions. *Criminal Justice Policy Review* 10: 491-502.

Ruddell, Rick and Matthew Thomas. 2010. "Minority Threat and Police Strength: An Examination of the Golden State." *Police Practice and Research* 11(3): 256-273.

Rumbaut, R.G., Gonzales, R.G., Golnaz. K., Morgan, C.V., Tafoya-Estrada, R. 2006. "Immigration and Incarceration." In: Martinez R., and A. Valenzuela, eds., *Immigration and Crime*. New York: NYU Press.

Russell-Brown, K. (2009). *The color of crime* (2nd ed). New York: New York University Press.

Sakamoto, A., Huei-Hwsia, Wu, and J.M. Tzeng. 2000. The Declining Significance of Race Among American Men in the Latter Half of the 20th Century." *Demography* 37(1): 41-50.

Sampson, Robert J. 1986. "Effects of Socioeconomic Context on Official Reaction to Juvenile Delinquency." *American Sociological Review* 51(6): 876-885.

Sampson, R. J. and Bartusch, D. J. 1998. "Legal Cynicism and (Subcultural?) Tolerance of Deviance: The Neighborhood Context of Racial Differences." *Law and Society Review* 32: 777-804.

Sampson, Robert and Lydia Bean. 2006. "Cultural Mechanisms and Killing Fields: A Revised Theory of Community-Level Racial Inequality" In: Ruth Peterson, Lauren Krivo and John Hagan, eds., *The Many Colors of Crime: Inequalities of Race, Ethnicity and Crime in America*. New York: NYU Press.

Sampson, Robert J. and W. Byron Groves. 1989. "Community Structure and Crime: Testing Social Disorganization Theory." *American Journal of Sociology* 94: 774-802.

Sampson, R., Jeffrey D. Morenoff, and Stephen W. Raudenbush. 2005. "Social anatomy of racial and ethnic disparities in violence." *American Journal of Public Health* 95(2): 225-32.

Sanchez-Jankowski, Martin. 1991. *Islands in the Street: Gangs and American Urban Society*. Berkeley: University of California Press.

Sealock, Miriam and Sally S. Simpson. 1998. "Unraveling Bias in Arrest Decisions: The Role of Juvenile Offender Type-Scripts." *Justice Quarterly* 15(3): 427-457.

Sellin, Thorstein. 1938. *Culture, Conflict, and Crime*. Social science research council: New York.

Shannon, Lyle. 1991. *Changing Patterns of Delinquency and Crime*. Boulder, CO: Westview Press.

Shaw, Clifford, and Henry McKay. 1942. *Juvenile Delinquency and Urban Areas*. Chicago: University of Chicago Press.

Short, J.F. Jr. and F. I. Nye. 1957. "Reported Behavior as a Criterion of Deviant Behavior." *Social Problems* 5: 207-213.

Short, James, and Fred Strodtbeck. 1965. *Group Process and Gang Delinquency*. Chicago: University of Chicago Press.

Simcha-Fagan, Ora, and Joseph E. Schwartz. 1986. "Neighborhood and Delinquency: An Assessment of Contextual Effects." *Criminology* 24: 667-703

Sissons, Peter. 1979. *The Hispanic Experience of Criminal Justice*. Hispanic Research Center: Fordham University, Bronx, NY. Monograph Series.

Smith, Doug. 1986. "The neighborhood context of police behavior." In: Albert Reiss and Michael Tonry, eds., *Crime and Justice, vol 8*. Chicago: University of Chicago Press.

Smith, Doug and Christy Visher. 1981. "Street-level justice: situational determinants of police arrest decisions." *Social Problems* 29(2): 167-177.

Snyder, Howard. 1999. "Juvenile Arrest 1998" *OJJDP Bulletin*, NCJ 179064

Snyder, Howard. 2002. "Juvenile Arrest 2000" *OJJDP Bulletin*, NCJ 191729

Snyder, Howard. 2006. "Juvenile Arrest 2004" *OJJDP Bulletin*, December: 1-12.

Snyder, Howard. 2008. "Juvenile Arrest 2007" *OJJDP Bulletin*, NCJ 221338.

Steffensmeier, D., Schwartz, J., Zhong, H. and J. Ackerman. 2005. "An assessment of recent trend in girls' violence using diverse longitudinal sources: is the gender gap closing?" *Criminology* 43(2): 355-406.

Stinchcombe, Arthur. 1963. "Institutions of privacy in the determination of police administrative practice." *American Journal of Sociology* 69(2): 150-160.

Sutherland, Edwin. H. and Donald Cressey 1978. "The Theory of Differential Association." *Criminology, 10th Edition*, New York: Harper & Row.

Sweeten, Gary. 2006. ""Who will graduate?: Disruption of High School education by arrest and court involvement." *Justice Quarterly* 23(4): 462-480.

Sweeten, G., Bushway, S., and Paternoster, R. 2009. Does dropping out of school mean dropping into delinquency? *Criminology* 47: 47-91.

Tannenbaum, Frank. 1938. *Crime and the Community*. Atheneum Press: Boston.

Tapia, M., and P. M. Harris. 2006. "Race and Revocation: Is There a Penalty for Young, Minority Males?" *Journal of Ethnicity in Criminal Justice* 4(3): 1–24.

Tapia, Mike. 2010. "Untangling race and class effects in juvenile arrest." *Journal of Criminal Justice, 38, 3, 255-265.*

Terry, Robert. 1967. "Discrimination in the Handling of Juvenile Offenders by social control agencies." *Journal of Research in Crime and Delinquency* 4: 218-230.

Thompson, Kevin, David Brownfield, and Anne Sorensen. 1996. "Specialization Patterns of Gang and Nongang Offending: A Latent Structure Analysis." *Journal of Gang Research* 3(3): 25-35.

Thornberry, Terrence P. 1987. "Toward an Interactional Theory of Delinquency." *Criminology* 25(4): 863-87.

Thornberry T.P. and Marvin D. Krohn. 2002. "Comparison of self-report and official data for measuring crime." pp. 43-94 in: Pepper JV, Petrie CV, eds., *Measurement Problems in Criminal Justice Research: Workshop Summary.* Washington, DC: National Academies Press. 2002.

Thornberry T.P., M.D. Krohn, A.J. Lizotte, and D. Chard-Wierchem. 1993. "The Role of Juvenile Gangs in Facilitating Delinquent Behavior." *Journal of Research in Crime and Delinquency* 30(1): 55-87.

Thornberry T.P., Krohn MD, A.J. Lizotte, C.A. Smith, and K. Tobin. 2003 *Gangs and Delinquency in Developmental Perspective.* New York: Cambridge University Press.

Thrasher, Frederick. 1927. *The Gang.* Chicago: The University of Chicago Press.

Tielman, K.S. and P.H. Landry. 1981. "Gender Bias in Juvenile Justice." *Journal of Research in Crime and Delinquency*, January: 47-80.

Tracy, Paul. 1979. *Subcultural Delinquency: Comparison of Incidence and Seriousness of Gang and Non-Gang Member Offensivity*. Philadelphia, University of Pennsylvania Center for Studies in Criminology and Criminal Law.

Tracy, Paul, Kempf-Leonard, Kimberly, and Stephanie Abramoske-James. 2009. "Gender Differences in Delinquency and Juvenile Justice Processing." *Crime and Delinquency* 55(2): 171-215.

Turk, Austin. 1969. *Criminality and the Legal Order*. Chicago: Rand McNally.

Uniform Crime Report. 1995-2005. Federal Bureau of Investigation. www.fbi.gov

Urbina, Martin G. 2007. Latino/as in the criminal and juvenile justice systems. *Critical Criminology 15*(1): 41-99.

U.S. Census Bureau 2010. Population Estimates. http://www.census. gov/popest/national/asrh/ accessed 6/1/2010.

Valdez, Al. 2000. *Gangs: A Guide to Understanding Street Gangs*, 3rd ed. San Clemente, CA: Law Tech Publishing.

Valdez, Avelardo. 2006. "Drug Markets in Minority Communities: Consequences for Mexican American Youth Gangs." In: Ruth Peterson, Lauren Krivo and John Hagan, eds, *The Many Colors of Crime: Inequalities of Race, Ethnicity and Crime in America*. New York: NYU Press.

Valdez, A., Mikow, J. and Cepeda, A. 2006. The Role of Stress, Family Coping, Ethnic Identity and Mother-Daughter Relationships on Substance Use among Gang Affiliated Hispanic Females." *Journal of Social Work Addictions* 6(4) 31-54.

Velez, Maria. 2006. "Lower Rates of Homicide in Latino versus Black Neighborhoods," In: Ruth Peterson, Lauren Krivo and John Hagan, eds, *The Many Colors of Crime: Inequalities of Race, Ethnicity and Crime in America*. New York: NYU Press

Velez, Maria 2009. "Contextualizing the Immigration and Crime Effect: An Analysis of Homicide in Chicago Neighborhoods." *Homicide Studies* 13(3): 325-335.

Veysey, Bonita M. and Steven F. Messner. 1999. "Further Testing of Social Disorganization Theory: An Elaboration of Sampson and Groves 'Community Structure and Crime.'" *Journal of Research in Crime and Delinquency* 36: 156-174.

Vigil, James Diego. 1988. *Barrio Gangs: Street Life and Identity in Southern California*. Austin: Texas University Press.

Vigil, James Diego. 2002. *A Rainbow of Gangs: Street Cultures in the Mega-City*. Austin: Texas University Press.

Vito, G., and Walsh, W. 2008. "Suspicion and traffic stops: Crime control or racial profiling?" *International Journal of Police Science and Management 10*: 89-100.

Walker, Samuel, Cassia Spohn, and Miriam DeLone. 2003. *The Color of Justice: Race, Ethnicity and Crime in America*. Beverly, MA: Wadsworth.

Walker, N. E., Senger, J. M., Villarruel, F. A. Arboleda, A. 2004. *Lost Opportunities: The reality of Latinos in the U.S. Criminal Justice System.* Washington, DC: National Council of La Raza.

Warr, Mark and Mark Stafford. 1991. "The Influence of Delinquent Peers: What They Think or What They Do?" *Criminology* 29: 851-866.

Warr, Mark. 1996. "Organization and instigation in delinquent groups." *Criminology* 34(1): 11-37.

Warr, Mark. 2002. *Companions in Crime: The social aspects of criminal conduct.* New York: Cambridge University Press.

Watt, Toni, and J.M. Rogers 2007. "Factors Contributing to Differences in Substance Abuse Among Black and White Adolescents." *Youth and Society* 39(1): 54-74.

Weiner, Normal L., and Charles V. Willie. 1971. "Decisions by Juvenile Officers." The *American Journal of Sociology* 77(2): 199-210.

Weisheit, Ralph, and Edward Wells. 2004. "Youth Gangs in Rural America." *National Institute of Justice Journal* 251: 1-5.

Werthman, Carl and Irving Piliavin. 1967. "Gang members and the police." In: Bordua, ed., *The Police: Six Sociological Essays.* New York: Wiley and Sons.

Western, Bruce. 2006. *Punishment and Inequality in America.* New York, Russell Sage Foundation.

Wilbanks, William 1987. *The Myth of a Racist Criminal Justice System.* Monterey, CA: Brooks/Cole.

Williams, J. R. and M. Gold. 1972. "From Delinquent Behavior to Official Delinquency." *Social Problems* 20(2): 209-229.

Wilson, George. 2000. "Income in Upper-Tier Occupations Among Males Over the 1st Decade of the Work Career: Is Race Declining in Significance." *National Journal of Sociology* 12(1): 105-128.

Wikstrom, Per-Olof and Rolf Loeber. 2000. "Do Disadvantaged Neighborhoods Cause Well-Adjusted Children to Become Adolescent Delinquents? A study of male juvenile serious offending, individual risk and protective factors, and neighborhood context." *Criminology* 38(4): 1109-1143.

Winfrey, Thomas, Backstrom, Theresa, and Larry Mays. 1994. "Social Learning Theory, Self Reported Delinquency, and Youth Gangs." *Youth and Society* 26(2): 147-177.

Wooldridge, Jeffrey. 2002. *Econometric Analysis of Cross Section and Panel Data.* Cambridge, MA: MIT Press.

Worden, Robert E., Shepard, Robin, and Mastrofski, Stephen. 1996. "On the meaning and Measurement of Suspect's Demeanor toward police: A Comment on 'Demeanor and Arrest'." *Journal of Research in Crime and Delinquency* 33(3): 324-332.

Wordes, M. and Bynum, T.S. 1995. "Policing juveniles: is there bias against youths of color?" in Kemph-Leonard, Pope, and Feyerherm, eds., *Minorities in juvenile justice.* Thousand Oaks, Calif. : Sage.

Zatz, Margerie. 1985. "Los Cholos: Legal Processing of Chicano Gang Members." *Social Problems* 33: 13-30.

Zatz, Margerie. 1987. "Chicano youth gangs and crime, creation of a moral panic." *Contemporary Crises* 11: 129-158.

Index

age, 37
  as demographic control,
    69
  higher age groups, 132
  link to prior arrests, 86
  study cohorts, 61
alcohol use, 31, 62, 66,
  75, 87
arrest
  bias, 36, 51, 74, 85, 89
  data, 2, 10, 12, 16, 19,
    21
  Hispanics, 24
  predictors, 15, 23, 27,
    29, 31, 33, 38, 51, 65,
    86–89, 110
  records, 17, 31, 32, 33,
    62, 68, 69, 76, 80,
    123
arson, 29
Asian Americans, 64
assault, 31, 66, 75, 88,
  132, 134
Bell, Duran, 4, 16, 18, 25,
  34, 52, 62, 85, 131

Black, Donald, 3, 6, 8,
  16, 18, 20, 23, 26, 28,
  29, 34, 38, 84, 131
Briar, Scott, 18, 20, 21,
  23, 28, 34, 38, 62, 131
Bureau of Labor
  Statistics, 60
Census data, 27, 123
Center for Human
  Resource Research, 61
Charlotte, NC, 26
Chicago, IL, 45, 46, 56,
  107
Cleveland, OH, 44
conditional effects, 53,
  96, 119
conflict theory, 3–14, 119
counsel and release, 20,
  34, 62
crime prevalence, 30
crime severity, 28–30, 38,
  65
criminal history, 32, 38,
  65
curfew violations, 25, 75

Curry, David, 2, 3, 11, 16, 17, 19, 33, 45, 48, 49, 56, 57, 68, 80, 107, 128

Dannefur, Dale, 16, 21, 23, 25, 29, 34, 35, 52, 85

data
  arrest, 23–32, 37, 46, 49, 60, 61, 64
  literature, 8, 12, 13, 15, 21, 22, 21–30, 35, 36, 41, 44, 48, 51, 57, 67, 69, 72, 75, 80, 91, 95, 103, 120, 124

demeanor, 20, 23

Denver, CO, 44

differential association, 59

differential involvement, 3, 66, 80

differential selection, 3

differential treatment, 7, 53, 78, 119, 123, 131, 134, *See also* racial profiling

disproportionate minority contact (DMC), 13, 85, 89, 133

drug crimes, 29, 31, 87, 132

drug dealing, 58, 67, 75

drug sales, 66, 80, 110, *See*

drug use, 66, 75, 110

Dunford, F., 16, 17, 20, 32, 34, 59, 129

Elliott, Delbert, 16

exaggeration, 67

gangs
  civil injunctions, 9, 39, 49, 117
  definition, 65
  in rural areas, 69
  membership, 2, 10, 9–14, 41–49, 55–60, 80, 81, 103–18, 126–30
  subculture, 9, 11, 43, 107
  turf, 11, 42, 58, 65
  wannabe, 56, 104

geographic place, 61, 69

Hirschfield, Paul, 2, 8, 16, 19, 21, 23, 25, 27, 31, 35, 52, 62, 76, 86, 89, 133

hypotheses, study, 52–60

hypothesis, intuitive, 118

hypothesis, paradoxical, 115

income, household, 61, 65, 72, 78, 92–101, 95, 96, 110, 124, 125

interaction effects, 11, 29,
55, 57, 73, 95, 110,
124, 129
labeling theory, 3–14, 26,
33, 49, 51, 73, 74, 84,
85, 103, 120
Lang, Kevin, 4, 16, 18,
25, 34, 52, 62, 85, 131
larceny, 28, 36
Latino Paradox, 54
Lundman, Richard, 1, 3,
6, 16, 18, 20, 21, 23,
26, 28, 29, 38, 84, 131
marginalization, 4, 5, 43,
130
multiple, 57
marijuana use, 31, 66,
104
McKay, Henry, 12, 41,
42, 57, 128
mediation effects, 92, 95,
107, 110, 119, 124
Mexican Americans, 25,
85
middle class, 5, 7
minorities, ethnic, 5, 12,
22–26
minorities, racial, 5, 12,
22–26
misdemeanors, 29
Monahan, Thomas, 17,
18, 21, 26, 28, 29, 33,
35, 36, 38, 64, 68, 69,
131
Nagin, Daniel, 21, 32, 33,
68
National Crime
Victimization Survey,
122
National Incident-Based
Reporting System, 122
National Longitudinal
Survey of Youth, 24,
60
National Survey of
Youth, 31
National Youth Survey,
32
neighborhood, 42
neighborhood boundaries,
59, 129
neighborhood
disadvantage, 23
out of place, 19, 54, 59,
80, 100, 116, 125, 129
phenotype, varying, 122
Philadelphia, PA, 28, 29,
64
Piliavin, Irving, 7, 9, 18,
19, 20, 21, 23, 28, 33,
34, 37, 38, 49, 55, 57,
59, 62, 68, 131
Pittsburgh, PA, 24
police contact, 6, 16–20

police contact data, 16–20, 28

police discretion, 6, 18, 67, 84, 85, 89

Pope, Carl, 16, 29, 32

population heterogeneity, 32, 42

poverty, 1, 7–8, 11, 27, 42, 51, 52, 54, 57, 59, 91, 101, 118, 125, 128

qualitative studies, 19, 57, 129

racial profiling, 5, 74, 119, 129, 131

random effects model (REM), 70

regression, 65, 96, 99, 100, 127

regression coefficients, 72, 131

regression, negative binomial, 70, 91

regression, Poisson, 104, 120

Reiss, Albert, 3, 6, 8, 16, 18, 20, 23, 26, 28, 29, 34, 38, 84, 131

Rochester, NY, 24, 45, 89

Safe Schools Act, 88

Sampson, Robert, 1, 2, 8, 12, 16, 17, 19, 21, 23, 27, 29, 31, 35, 42, 46, 52, 53, 54, 56, 60, 101, 125, 128

Schutt, Russell, 16, 21, 23, 25, 29, 34, 35, 52, 85

Seattle Youth Study, 46, 56

Seattle, WA, 24, 33, 44, 46, 56, 107

self report data, 16, 23, 26, 30, 37, 44, 75, 131, 133

Shaw, Clifford, 12, 41, 42, 57, 128

Snyder, Howard, 16, 29, 32

social class, 8, 11, 15, 19, 22, 26, 49, 53, 119, 128, 131

social correlates, 22, 41

social disorganization theory, 11, 124–31, 57

socioeconomic status (SES), 2, 26–28, 31, 73, 78, 80, 81, 91–101, 103–11, 115–17, 119, 121, 124–31

  interviewer-rated, 78

state-dependence, 32

status offense, 75

substance use, 30, 66, 80, 133

targeting, 6, 9, 11, 19, 25,
  26, 54, 73, 117, 119,
  123, 126, 127, 135
testing effects, 67
theft
  auto, 28, 42, 65
  grand, 75
  minor, 132
  petty, 75, 88

Uniform Crime Report,
  37, 122
vandalism, 66, 67, 75, 87,
  110, 132
Werthman, Carl, 7, 9, 18,
  19, 23, 33, 37, 49, 55,
  57, 59, 68, 131
witness statements, 131